Hatches, Matches and Dispatches

Also by Jenny Paschall and Ron Lyon

ODD LAWS

Hatches, Matches and Dispatches

BIRTH, MARRIAGE AND BURIAL
AROUND THE WORLD

Jenny Paschall
& Ron Lyon

HarperCollinsPublishers

HarperCollins*Publishers*
77–85 Fulham Palace Road,
Hammersmith, London W6 8JB

A Paperback Original 1997
1 3 5 7 9 8 6 4 2

A catalogue record for this book is
available from the British Library

ISBN 0 00 638815 9

Set in Berling by
Rowland Phototypesetting Ltd,
Bury St Edmunds, Suffolk

Printed and bound in Great Britain by
Caledonian International Book Manufacturing Ltd, Glasgow

WITH LOVE
TO CAMERON STEPHANIE LYON
Hatched on 14th August 1996

HATCHES

∽

Confusion – 1 Science – 0

I F the number of humans on planet Earth were to continue to increase at the current rate, by the year 3530 the total weight of all the living human bodies would equal the mass of the earth itself. Given the same rate of population expansion, by the year 6826, the total mass of humanity would equal the size of the entire known universe.

O N the other hand, Danish researchers have found that men's average sperm count has almost halved over the past fifty years, and that semen quantity has decreased by almost twenty-five per cent. Similar results are being found in tests being conducted in other parts of the world. So far, no one has been able to identify the cause. Scientists are concerned that if this trend continues, it could lead ultimately to a sterile population.

P ERHAPS man's diminishing fertility is caused by his first love, the car.
Driving for more than three hours a day can reduce a man's fertility. Scientists have discovered that driving a car and sitting

in traffic jams, especially whilst wearing tight-fitting clothes and underpants, causes overheating of the testes, which reduces the output of sperm.

However, it seems that if a good part of a man's day is spent overheating his testes, he may be able to counteract the problem by drinking plenty of coffee. According to doctors at New York University Medical School, the caffeine in coffee prolongs the life span of male sperm and keeps them moving.

Eggcentric Tales

All the female eggs needed to produce the next generation of the human race can be contained within the shell of one chicken's egg.

In 1982 Lee Perry, a female Harvard university professor, sued Dr Richard Atkinson, chancellor of the University of California at San Diego, because he refused to make her pregnant. She volunteered to abandon the case in exchange for Dr Atkinson's sperm.

According to research in Norway, eggs are an aphrodisiac. In a study of men with low libidos, it was found that eighty-four per cent felt an increase in sexual desire after being treated with an extract from fertilized chickens' eggs. Soft lights, music, wine and ... scrambled eggs? We'll stick with oysters!

WHEN a 5,000-year-old man was found preserved in ice in the Alps, researchers at Austria's Innsbruck University were inundated with calls from women who wanted to be artificially inseminated with the sperm of the original Mr Cool.

IN 1863, during the United States Civil War, a woman was artificially inseminated by a bullet. While watching a battle from her front porch, with her mother and sister, this young lady was wounded in the abdomen by a stray bullet, which had already hit a soldier in his scrotum.

Both the soldier and the girl recovered. Nine months later, the girl delivered a baby boy, who closely resembled the young soldier. The surgeon who treated them both, Captain L. G. Capers, hypothesized that the bullet that struck the soldier carried the sperm into the young woman's uterus, thereby causing her to conceive. Following this discovery, the soldier and the young woman were formally introduced, fell in love and married. They had two more children, using less dramatic methods of conception.

ANOTHER unusual long-distance conception occurred in Sydney, Australia in 1969, when a fifteen-year-old schoolgirl claimed she had become pregnant after swimming in a public pool. Doctors confirmed the pregnant girl was a virgin, and the courts ruled that she had been impregnated by sperm in the swimming pool water.

ACCORDING to the World Health Organization, the sex act takes place at least 100 million times a day. This figure was computed by multiplying the world birth rate by the accepted estimate of the number of times sex does not result in conception.

THE largest cell in the human body is the female ovum, and the smallest is the male sperm. One egg cell weighs the same as 175,000 sperm.

To Be or Not To Be

THERE are 75 million volunteer workers on the China Family Planning Association.

A 1983 study showed that half of all pregnancies are mistakes.

ONE of the earliest methods of contraception, found on Egyptian papyrus dating from approximately 1850 BC, was a mixture of honey, soda, crocodile excrement, and some kind of gum, inserted into the vagina. It is uncertain whether it was supposed to kill sperm, or just destroy the man's urge to proceed!

THE first contraceptive diaphragms were citrus rinds.

JULIUS Caesar was so worried about the falling population of Rome, that he offered rewards to Romans for producing numerous children. Conversely, he punished childless women, by forbidding them to ride in carriages or wear jewellery.

UNTIL the beginning of the twentieth century, it was customary for a Muslim peasant woman in Upper Egypt to terminate an unwanted pregnancy by lying face down between railway tracks until a train came and passed over her. Conversely, women who had difficulty conceiving would lie on their backs in the belief that as the train passed over them, they would be impregnated. Trains were also thought to represent fertility in India, where women trying to conceive would rush to the tracks as a train approached. As the train rushed past, they would lift their skirts in the hope of being made pregnant.

LOVE may be blind, but it's not heat resistant. The lowest number of babies are born in April and May because temperatures in July and August are too hot for romance. The peak months for births are August and September. In heat wave years, the birth rate drops even more dramatically than the average April and May figures.

THE human female is the only animal capable of constant sexual arousal and is physically capable of making love every day of her adult life.

CASANOVA, one of the world's greatest lovers, boasted that England was the most sexually wild country. He also claimed he preferred to use British condoms.

DAN Patrick, general manager of Houston radio station KSEV, broadcast his regular morning talk show while undergoing a vasectomy.
When the show's producer said 'Cut!' – he really meant it!

IN the Yanomamo tribe, who live in Brazilian rain forests, a woman could kill her female babies until she gave birth to a son. Once she had borne a son, she could kill any further unwanted children.

IF music be the food of love . . . then why not try the singing condom? Invented by Hungarian Ferenc Kovacs, it begins to play immediately the condom is unrolled. The discerning user can choose one of two tunes: 'You Sweet Little Dumbbell', or 'Arise Ye Worker'.

Legal Tales

IN 1992 Dr Cecil B. Jacobson, the head of a fertility clinic in Vienna, Virginia, was convicted of fraud and perjury. Jacobson had been found to have used his own sperm to impregnate as many as seventy-five women, while telling his clients that the sperm was from anonymous donors.

WHEN a condom manufacturer decided to call his new range 'Stealth Condoms', the Northrop Corporation, builder of the B–2 Stealth Bomber, filed suit, claiming that people might confuse the two products!

ONE of fourteen death row inmates in California who filed a lawsuit asking the state to allow them to father children either through conjugal visits or artificial insemination was a certain gentleman named Herbert J. Coddington. His crime? Killing his two children following a custody dispute with his wife.

Baby Facts

BABIES can breathe and swallow at the same time – adults cannot.

WHEN babies are first born they have 350 bones in their bodies. Adults have only 206 bones as some fuse together as a baby grows up.

A NEW-BORN baby's body is only twenty per cent of its adult size, while its brain is ninety per cent of its adult volume.

WHEN a baby is born, it has many more taste buds than its mother. It will be able to distinguish its mother's milk from that of a stranger soon after birth.

STATISTICALLY, a baby born in Singapore or Hong Kong is more likely to survive its first year than a baby born in the USA.

A three-month-old foetus already has the fingerprints it will have for the rest of its life.

AT four months, a foetus can frown.

100,000 nerve cells sprout every minute after conception until, by birth, there are one billion.

Womb for Improvement

WHEN the Japanese obstetrician, Dr Hajime Murooka, investigated the reasons why babies cry, he came to the conclusion that some are just homesick for the womb they have recently left. He implanted a tiny microphone in the uterus of a pregnant woman and recorded the sounds within. When these amplified sounds were played to crying babies, in almost all cases, the crying stopped. One Florida hospital was so impressed with the results that the sounds were piped into a maternity ward. Not only did the babies seem quieter, but the mothers and staff felt calm and drowsy.

SCIENTISTS have found hints of consciousness in seven-month-old foetuses still in the uterus, and have measured brain wave patterns like those during dreaming in eight-month-olds. After twenty-eight weeks *in utero*, the foetus can hear. By the third trimester, the foetus can respond to sound. Car horns make the foetus jump. Research in Belfast found that the theme song from a popular soap opera, played repeatedly to thirty-week foetuses, made them relaxed. When the same music was played after birth, the babies became more alert.

THERE are a number of electronic devices available in the United States which ensure that pre-school learning begins pre-birth. The Uterine University offers 'Foetal Teaching Systems' – cassettes to be worn by the pregnant woman on a body belt, available from a Mr Shannon Thomas of Orlando, Florida. Also available is the 'Listen Baby' fabric belt with two speakers and a little microphone, from Roger Hurst of Infant Technology in Denver, and the 'Pregaphone', invented by Dr Rene Van de Carr of Santa Barbara, California.

Birthdays

KING John III of Poland was born on 17 June – he was married on 17 June, crowned on 17 June, and died on 17 June. In short 17 June was the day on which he was hatched, matched, dispatched.

What's in a Name?

UNTIL the 1970s, French families were not free to choose just any name for their children – they had to pick names from an official list kept by the Ministry of the Interior.

IN ancient Rome, naming children was pretty difficult too – there were only twenty first names ever used for males.

MUHAMMAD is the most common first name in the world, Chang is the most common surname. We have yet to find a Muhammad Chang though!

BRIAN Brown of Wolverhampton was such a big boxing fan that when his daughter was born in 1974, he named her after twenty-five world heavyweight champions – Maria Sullivan Corbett Fitzsimmons Jeffries Hart Burns Johnson Willard Dempsey Tunney Schmeling Sharkey Carnera Baer Braddock Louis Charles Walcott Marciano Patterson Johanssen Liston Clay Frazier Foreman Brown.

EQUALLY unfortunate was the daughter of Peter O'Sullivan, a fan of the Liverpool football team of the sixties. When she was born, her proud dad named her after the entire team: Paula St John Lawrence Lawler Byrne Strong Yeats Stevenson Callaghan Hunt Milne Smith Thompson Shankly Bennett Paisley O'Sullivan. On official documents, she used the name Paula St John etc O'Sullivan.

A Japanese couple who won a free honeymoon courtesy of the German airline Lufthansa were so grateful for their wonderful trip to Germany and their romantic stay in the Black Forest that when their son was born nine months later, they named him 'Lufthansa'.

ARTHUR Pepper had his daughter christened in 1883, with the name Anna Bertha Cecilia Diana Emily Fanny Gertrude Hypatia Inez Jane Kate Louisa Maud Nora Ophelia Quince Rebecca Sarah Teresa Ulysses Venus Winifred Xenophon Yetty Zeus Pepper – one name for every letter of the alphabet.

MR and Mrs James Williams felt that their own names were pretty uninspired, so when their daughter was born on 12 September 1984 in Beaumont, Texas, they named her: Roshandiatellyneshiaunneveshenkkoyaanfsquatsiuty.

ON 8 November 1847, Dr James Young Simpson, professor of midwifery at Edinburgh University, first used chloroform as an anaesthetic in the delivery of the wife of a fellow surgeon. She was so delighted with the painless delivery that she named her daughter Anaesthesia.

IN 1971 Grace Slick officially named her daughter 'god'. When she was asked why she registered the name with a small g, she replied, 'Because we've got to be humble about this.'

Bottoms Up

IN the UK, 2,191,781 pounds of paper are used in non-recyclable disposable nappies every year. 48,835,616 disposable nappies are thrown away.

JAPANESE mothers change their babies' nappies an average of fourteen times a day – twice as much as European and American mothers.

SAINSBURY'S once promised a year's supply of free nappies for pregnant mums whose waters break in one of their stores.

SOME professions pose problems that we lesser mortals thankfully never have to worry about. Take, for instance, nappy manufacturers. How do they test their products? It seems that babies can be unreliable when it comes to delivering waste on time, so scientists at the Kimberley Clark Corporation have come up with synthetic faeces. Apparently testers, reluctant to use the real thing, had tried mashed potatoes, peanut butter, and even tinned pumpkin pie mix – but none of them was chemically accurate enough.

Delighted testers can now use a compound which comes in a dry mix to which water is added for the desired consistency. It can be any colour, but they usually use brown. At the request of the testers, it is odourless. For anyone interested in the recipe, the US patent number is 5,356,626.

AMERICAN parents can make potty training fun by purchasing an audio book entitled 'I'm on the Potty'. Set to familiar nursery rhyme tunes, they can sing along with 'Diapers Falling on the Ground' (Instead of 'London Bridge is Falling Down'), and 'I'm on the Potty'. Presumably, 'Raindrops Keep Falling on My Head' is not included, although we thought we might suggest 'Spending Pennies From Heaven' for the next edition.

Quotable Quotes

'The first half of our lives is ruined by our parents and the second half by our children.'   *Clarence Darrow*

'An ugly baby is a very nasty object, and the prettiest is frightful when undressed.'   *Queen Victoria*

'The thing that impresses me most about America is the way parents obey their children.' *Duke of Windsor*

Royal Babies – and Their Parents

PRINCE Hartmann of Liechtenstein, 1613–86, had twenty-four children – more than any other royal parent. Duke Roberto of Parma, 1848–1907, also had twenty-four children – but by two different wives.

ANAESTHESIA was originally opposed by churchmen as a method to ease the pain of childbirth. They claimed that in the Bible, Eve was told, 'In sorrow thou shalt bring forth children' as a punishment for eating the forbidden fruit, and that it was going against God's will to ensure painless childbirth. However, when Queen Victoria benefited from its effects during the birth of her seventh child in 1853, churchmen suddenly decided that maybe it was not a sin after all. Thereafter, it was known as 'anaesthesia à la Reine'.

MARIE Antoinette was a trend-setter in the eighteenth century, and all the fashionable ladies at court would study and copy everything she wore. When she became pregnant, the ladies followed her trend – not by conceiving, but by inserting ever larger cushions under their clothes as the queen's pregnancy progressed. Not surprisingly, as soon as Marie Antoinette gave birth to the Dauphin, the padded stomach became last season's look!

WHEN British royal babies are christened, holy water from the River Jordan is specially flown in. The font is brought in from the Jewel House of the Tower of London for the occasion, and the cream Honiton lace christening gown bears the needlework of the young Edward VII, who was reputed to have taken four hours to fashion each square inch of the garment's wild rose pattern.

Superstitions

UP until the late Victorian period, people believed that a suckling baby absorbed the moral character of the woman nursing. So, if a mother could not breast-feed her own child, the wet nurse was subject to a rigorous cross-examination on her morality. If the parents suspected she was a drunkard, or a half-wit, they believed the child would be one too.

THE Chinook Indian tribe considered a flat skull to be a sign of beauty – so they strapped babies head to toe between boards until the end of their first year.

THE significance of storks in connection with babies seems to emanate from beliefs spanning many centuries and cultures. In Roman mythology, the stork was sacred to Venus, the goddess of love, so the ancients considered it a sign of good luck if storks nested near their home. The stork has long been considered a good luck omen in Norse, German and Dutch folklore.

IN nineteenth-century Wales, the bone from a shoulder of mutton was used to predict the sex of an unborn child. After being charred in a fire, the bone was hung over the door of the house. It was believed that the child would be the same sex as the next person to come through the door.

IN Germany it was once believed that a wife who carried one of her husband's socks would never give birth prematurely.

A baby born into the Akha tribe of Thailand cannot be touched until it has cried three times.

THE Asmat people of New Guinea believe that, in order to have a baby, a woman must be impregnated by the spirit of an ancestor and the spirit is always of the same sex as the new-born child.

IN some African tribes, the men will take to their beds for the entire duration of their wife's pregnancy. The women continue to work as usual until a few hours before giving birth. They believe that men are cleverer as well as physically stronger than women and are therefore better able to defend unborn children against malign and evil spirits.

THE Punan tribe of Borneo believe that women are born without a soul, and do not acquire one until they marry. There are certain advantages to this – as she has no soul, she cannot sin, so Punan girls can have a very active sex life until they marry. There is, however, a drawback to this belief. In order to gain a soul, the Punan girl's husband has to find her

---

one. He goes off into the jungle, and returns some days later with a severed human head. This is tied to the head of the bride, and the medicine man performs various rites lasting several days until everyone is satisfied that the soul has transferred from the head to the girl.

I N medieval Europe a woman would put on her husband's clothes when labour started, hoping to transfer the birth pains to him.

The medieval belief that all fathers felt sympathetic pains when their children were born could get men in hot water. Villagers in the north of England would seek out the father of an illegitimate child simply by waiting for the mother to go into labour, and then scouring the village for any man lying ill in bed.

T HERE is a strange myth that a premature baby of seven months has a better chance of survival than one of eight months. While it is now obvious that the longer the baby is in the uterus, the stronger it will be, this myth survives. It is believed that the idea originated with astrologers, to whom seven was a magic number.

Adoption

P ERHAPS no other society honours friendship with the unselfishness of the Hawaiians. Those who are blessed with infants give them to those who are not, a practice known as *hanai*. *Hanai* takes place between close friends and family, the children know who their genetic parents are and see them regularly. The children are considered temporary gifts, not possessions.

T HE first record of adoption by childless couples has been found in ancient Sumerian law codes dating from 1800 BC. The laws enabled childless couples to adopt a child so that their worldly possessions could be passed to an heir.

Be Fruitful and Multiply

T HE world's heaviest twins weighed in collectively at twenty-seven pounds and twelve ounces, and were born to Mrs J. P. Haskin of Fort Smith, Arizona, in 1924.

I N 1994, Cynthia Silveira gave birth to two healthy girls eight days apart, one from each of her two uteri. One in 50,000 women have two uteri, but the cases of pregnancy in both uteri in which the mother gave birth vaginally are astronomically rare.

M ADISON Barbara, Jackson Frederick and Allison Rose-marie are a little different from most triplets. They were born to two women in different cities, and in different years.
When their parents, Linda and Marty Schaper, discovered it was unlikely they could have children of their own, Linda's sister, Barb, suggested a plan. If they both had embryos implanted, it would increase the chances of Linda having children. Marty and Linda would be the biological parents, Linda would still have a chance of giving birth to her own child, but

Barb, who already had a family, could be a surrogate mother. Both sisters underwent IVF – which was successful for both of them. Linda gave birth to her own twins in St Louis, on Christmas Day 1993, and Barb gave birth to the third triplet, Allison, in Columbia, Missouri on 25 January 1994.

ANOTHER unusual set of twins are Hanna and Eric Lynn, who were born ninety-four days apart. Pegge Lynn, who lives in Pennsylvania, gave birth first to Hanna, who was almost four months premature, on 10 November 1995. She weighed just twenty-three ounces. Doctors stitched Mrs Lynn's cervix and gave her drugs to stop her labour progressing, and delay the delivery of the second twin as long as possible. They were incredibly successful – Eric was finally born on 2 February 1996, weighing a much healthier five pounds and seven ounces.

THIRTY-TWO-YEAR-OLD Czech Siamese twins Josepha and Rosa Blazek were admitted to hospital so that Rosa could give birth to her baby son. The father admitted paternity and was eager to marry Rosa, but he was told that if he did so, the Czech police would arrest him for bigamy as soon as the ceremony was over, so the son was registered as illegitimate.

TWO record-breakingly prolific women have each produced sixty-nine children. Mrs Fyodor Vassilet, a Russian, had sixty-nine babies in twenty-seven confinements – four sets of quadruplets, seven sets of triplets, and sixteen pairs of twins. She became extremely famous, and appeared at the court of Czar Alexander II. She died in 1872.

Her rival for the record, Mrs Bernard Schenberg of Austria, also had twenty-seven confinements, with four sets of quadruplets, seven sets of triplets, and sixteen pairs of twins. When she died in 1911, at the age of fifty-six, her husband Bernard remarried, and had a further eighteen children with his second wife.

THE most prolific mother living is Leontina Albina, born in 1925 in San Antonio, Chile, who gave birth to her fifty-fifth child in 1981. Amongst the births were five sets of triplets. Only forty children survived.

IN 1993, a woman who had been treated at one of the most prestigious fertility clinics in the Netherlands gave birth to twin sons – one black and one white. Both she and her partner, who had given his sperm for artificial insemination, are white. It seemed that a technician had reused a pipette that still contained some sperm from a previous insemination. DNA tests proved that the biological father of one of the twins is from the Caribbean island of Aruba.

GIOVANNI Aversa, an Italian living in Bristol, desperately wanted a son. After his wife Maria had given birth to two beautiful healthy daughters, they decided to try once more for a son. When Maria found she was expecting quadruplets, a delighted Giovanni was told that there was only a three million to one chance that his wife would have four daughters. At last, he was going to have his son to take to football matches. But, when Maria gave birth in March 1996 at the Southmead Hospital in Bristol, out came Giorgia, followed by Claudia, followed by Chiara, and finally Fabbrizia – four girls.

Unnatural Selection

FOR couples who are serious about sex selection, there are always the laboratory-based Sperm Olympics in Cleveland. Technicians put semen through various hurdles designed to separate the Y-bearing from X-bearing sperm. Laboratory methods take advantage of differences in weight, electrical charge and swimming speed to separate male from female sperm.

So far, they have apparently been correct fifty per cent of the time.

MORE than one in three couples who pay hundreds of pounds to chose the gender of their child at a controversial London fertility clinic end up with a baby of the opposite sex. The London Gender Clinic has estimated its success rates are more than fifty per cent but less than seventy per cent.

SUGAR and spice and all things nice, that's what little girls are made of. Slugs and snails and puppy dogs' tails, that's what little boys are made of. Well, not quite, but according to a study originally done in France, and followed up in Canada and Belgium, an eighty per cent success rate has been notched up by parents eating certain foods in order to conceive the favoured sex. The menu suggested for conceiving boys is: bananas, cherries, grapes, oranges, peaches, melons, raspberries, sprouts, celery, tomatoes and sweet corn. For girls, parents should try tangerines, grapefruit, apples, pineapples, pears, cucumbers, radishes, lettuce, cabbages, carrots, turnips.

But, one word of caution – anyone suffering from kidney problems should avoid the calcium-rich girl diet, and people with high blood pressure should pass up the salt-rich boy diet.

Designer Labels

B UNNY Hart and Sharon Barnett have come up with a range of designer swimwear for babies, which includes the 'Tarzan' for boys, and for girls the one-shoulder 'Jane', the 'Garbo', the 'Marilyn' and the 'Norma'. Their next collection will include tuxedo suits, and Lycra numbers which will be translucent except for appliqués of palm trees and flowers on strategic areas.

F OR the more daring babies, the latest in beach wear is the B-string - a G-string for kids. As a concession to sensitive stores, who were worried that a display of cheeks and nipples would be too much for some beach-loving parents, the designers of the B-string have created matching bandeaux, which can be worn as bikini tops. Alternatively, for those daring little Baywatch Babes under twelve months old, they can be worn as headbands.

B ABIES with style need money too – especially for a fancy outfit by Marc Bohan for Christian Dior. A saucy little number with a black velvet bustier, yellow satin puff skirt and tulle petticoat could set back the parents of the fashion addict a cool £2,500!

D ESIGNERS K. T. Maclay and Linda Sampson may have been the forerunners of the 'designer baby' concept. In 1972 in New York, they brought out a line of 'pregnancy puffs', strap-on, oval-shaped pillows that make the wearer look pregnant. Presumably, if a woman decided that pregnancy didn't suit her, she just adopted.

T HE Empathy Belly was created by Linda Ware, a prenatal educator from Washington. The belly consists of a huge womb-like structure with large breasts, costing £395 ($595). It is designed to be worn by the male partner so he can appreciate the discomfort of the late stages of pregnancy. It weighs thirty-five pounds and is guaranteed to cause backache, shortness of breath and fatigue. It also has a special pouch that presses on the wearer's bladder, creating a regular need to urinate.

Birth Tales

E VERY year, around eighty women go into labour on the New York subways, of which six or seven give birth on the platforms.

M AGDALENA Deskur and Maxine Arthur both work for *Sports Illustrated Magazine*. Although they are competitive, sporty women, who like to win, they had no idea they would be racing against each other – to give birth. They met in their obstetrician's office, where Maxine was found to be in labour, but nothing much seemed to be happening for Magdalena, who had thought she was in labour too. However, by the time Maxine had arrived at the admissions desk of the Beth Israel Hospital in New York, Magdalena's labour had started, and she was ready for admission at the same hospital. They went to their rooms in the same hallway, and their obstetrician began his own race – between the rooms of the two colleagues. At 6.19 p.m. Maxine gave birth to her seven-pound two-ounce son. Thirty-five minutes later, Magdalena produced a seven-pound-four-ounce girl. Both babies measured twenty inches. Exhausted Dr Swersky declared a photo finish.

I F Mary Ellen Allen had taken the time to have regular antenatal checks, the chances are that her daughter, Shadonna Allen, would never have been born. When Mary visited Dr James Lee, he discovered that her baby was growing outside Mrs Allen's Fallopian tubes, and had embedded itself in her abdominal cavity. As the unusual pregnancy was well advanced, however, he decided it was best to wait and see if the baby could survive. The chance was one in 200,000, but Shadonna was delivered eight weeks prematurely, weighing in at a tiny one pound and nine ounces.

T HE heaviest single birth on record was a boy weighing twenty-two pounds and eight ounces who was born to Signora Carmelina Fedele of Aversa, Italy in 1955.

Famous Babies

W HEN Pablo Picasso was born, the midwife thought he was stillborn, and left the baby lying on a table. His uncle, who was a doctor, saw the lifeless baby and decided to see if there was anything he could do. He tried mouth-to-mouth resuscitation, and young Pablo took his first breath.

L EONARDO da Vinci, Richard Wagner and Napoleon Bonaparte were all illegitimate.

T WENTY-ONE of the first twenty-three US astronauts who flew in space missions were either only children or firstborn sons, but no president of the US has been an only child.

W INSTON Churchill was born in a ladies' cloakroom. His mother had been attending a dance at Blenheim Palace when she went into premature labour.

M ARK Twain was born in 1835, when Halley's Comet appeared. And he died in 1910 – when it made its next appearance. Even more remarkable was his prediction years earlier: 'I was born when Halley's Comet came in, I will die when it comes back. It is fitting that these two freaks of nature should come in together, and go out together.'

Youngest . . .

M UM-ZI, a member of the harem of Chief Akkiri, ruler of the estuary of Calabar, Nigeria, became a mother at the age of eight years and four months. Her daughter followed in her precocious footsteps, and herself became a mother at the age of eight, making Mum-zi the youngest grandmother on record at the age of seventeen.

... And Oldest

A SIXTY-TWO-YEAR-OLD Italian woman, Rosanna Della Corte, gave birth on 18 July 1995 to a boy, Riccardo, in a Rome hospital. She had been impregnated by a donated egg that had been fertilized with sperm from her sixty-four-year-old husband.

Curiosities

M EDICAL science is giving new meaning to the phrase, 'putting something away for your child's future'. An increasing number of parents are putting away the blood from their baby's umbilical cord. The blood is being touted as an insurance policy families should have on hand in case their child contracts a life-threatening illness. The blood is collected from the placenta after the umbilical cord has been cut. It is tested for infection, then cryogenically frozen and stored in liquid nitrogen. The blood can be thawed and used to treat leukaemia, malignant tumours, immune diseases, anaemia, lymphoma, breast cancer and genetic disorders.

T HE Maternity Centre Association in New York organizes preparation classes for children who will be attending the birth of their siblings. They are taught about conception, birth, and how to change nappies.

O N an average day in the USA: 10,501 babies are born, and 5,937 people die. 178 babies are conceived by artificial insemination, of which ninety-six are conceived with sperm from a known donor, and forty are conceived with sperm from a sperm bank. 389 children are adopted, 1,994 babies are born to single mothers, 2,531 babies are born by Caesarean section. 217 sets of twins are born, five sets of triplets are born, ninety-eight babies are born away from a hospital, and 280 babies are delivered by midwives. 1,109,589 condoms are sold, of which 443,836 are purchased by women.

MATCHES

Courting Customs

D URING the reign of Queen Anne, St Valentine's Day was celebrated with an unusual game. Men put numbers in a bowl, and the women did the same. The numbers were then drawn and the men and women with the same numbers spent the day together, regardless of their marital status.

U NTIL the last century, 'bundling' was a normal part of courting among the Dutch and German immigrants in America. When a young man went courting, especially in the winter, the girl's parents would let him stay overnight in the same bed as their daughter, provided they both kept their clothes on, or bundled up in the bedcovers. There was a practical reason for this – the family did not have to burn precious wood in the evening, and the boy did not have to walk miles home on a cold night. Bundling boards were often used, which separated the couple while they were in bed. This custom still survives among the Amish in Pennsylvania.

W HEN a gentleman met a lady in public in eighteenth-century France, he was expected to kiss her on the neck.

I Thee Wed

MARRIAGE began in prehistoric times. When a man saw a woman he desired who was from another tribe, he would take her by force. These 'capture marriages' were legal in England until the thirteenth century. By that time, when the groom was going to abduct his chosen bride, he would take along his strongest friend or best warrior, in case of trouble with unco-operative relatives. This friend became known as 'the best man'.

Later, marriage became more of a trade between the groom and the father. The word 'wedd' meant the groom's pledge to marry in exchange for horses, land, cash, etc. The wedding was the actual exchange of goods. Sometimes the father of the bride would not let the groom see his intended for fear of the deal being cancelled if he disliked the look of her. So when the father gave his daughter away, the groom would lift the veil to see her face for the first time.

THE phrase 'tying the knot' comes from the ancient Celtic handfasting ceremony, in which the bride and groom were tied together at the hands.

IN ancient Greece, marriage was considered so essential for women that their age was counted from the date on which they were married to signify that the wedding marked the real beginning of life.

KOREAN women do not change their names after marriage.

Something Old, Something New

THE breaking of the glass in a Jewish wedding ceremony has many interpretations. For some, it signifies the frailty of human happiness, for others it refers to the destruction of the Israelite Temple in the year 70 AD. In the past, some Jewish husbands have insisted that it means they will have all the authority in the household.

IN some Rwandan and Tanzanian villages, the bride and groom face each other on their wedding day, seated on the lap of an elderly woman.

AT Armenian weddings, two white doves are released to signify love and happiness, while guests wrap the couple in a ribbon made of paper money during their first dance to ensure a lifetime of good fortune together.

THERE is an old tradition in Somerset in which the wedding party is locked in the churchyard and released only upon payment of a handful of coins.

YOUNG women in India's Karan tribe are given special lessons in the art of weeping – which they are only allowed to do on their wedding day.

THE American slave heritage is responsible for the interesting custom of 'jumping the broom'. Slaves were not legally entitled to have a Christian wedding ceremony, so although some ministers would marry them, it was not considered a legal marriage. Accordingly, the slaves invented their own ceremony, 'jumping the broom', which was based on the ancient African custom of jumping over a branch or tree trunk symbolizing the home. In the ceremony a circle is swept clean with the ritual broom, which is then laid out before the couple as they state their vows. Then, holding hands, they jump over the broom toward the east, the direction of beginnings.

The Always and Forever Wedding Chapel in Detroit now has a special 'jumping the broom service' available.

IN America it was once believed that the wedding ceremony should be completed between the half hour and the hour. The rising hand of the clock was said to denote success and rising fortune.

IN Iran, Syria, Cyprus, Turkey, India and parts of Europe, the bride and groom will each try to step on the other's toes. There is a belief that whoever does it first will be the one to rule the roost.

Young Love

THERE are a number of cultures in which the children are married off at a very early age. In the Fiji Islands children's marriages are arranged by their parents when they are three or four years old. Tasmanian wives are, as a rule, also betrothed to their husbands from infancy. Among certain Eskimo tribes, as soon as a girl is born, the young man who wants her for his wife makes an offer of marriage to the father of the infant.

But on Melville, an island off Australia, the Tiwi people go even further. They marry off girls before they have been conceived! The contract for the first-born daughter's future marriage is made at the mother's wedding ceremony.

I N Massachusetts, a girl can marry at twelve, but her husband must be at least fourteen years old.

Here Comes the Bride

I N Germany the bride's furniture was traditionally driven to her future home in a cart accompanied by musicians. At the threshold, she was greeted with a jug of beer offered by the groom; she, in turn, giving him a pair of shoes, a shirt she spun and wove, and the key to her bridal chest.

A T Egyptian weddings, the procession from the wedding to the reception is led by belly dancers, men carrying flaming swords, and people sounding long horns.

I N the Marquesas Islands, a bridegroom walks to his father-in-law's house on a human street formed by the prone wedding guests. He steps from back to back until he reaches his destination. At the altar the groom eats a raw fish that has been filleted and diced on a human body.

THE custom of tying old shoes to the back of the newly-weds' car comes from Hebraic history. The groom and the bride's father exchanged shoes at the wedding to symbolize her transfer to the new home. Similarly, in early Anglo-Saxon weddings, the bride's father handed the groom one of her slippers and the young husband would hit her over the head with it. This signified the passing of ownership from the father to the husband.

'Til Death Us Do Part

IF a Zulu tribesman is engaged to be married but dies before the wedding, his fiancée will marry one of his family who will father a child on the dead man's behalf.

IN ancient China, if the prospective groom met an untimely death, the bride would go ahead with the wedding cere-mony, marrying a ghost instead. She would then live with her dead husband's parents.

THE Hopi Indians of the south-western United States believe that marriage and death are fundamentally linked. The bride saves her wedding clothes for use as her funeral shroud. Without them her spirit cannot enter the afterworld.

Second Time Lucky

IN eighteenth-century America, a widow who was marrying again would stand naked in a cupboard and thrust her arm through a 'widow's hole' to her fully dressed groom. These nude, or 'shift' marriages symbolized that the widow brought only herself to the marriage, and none of her late husband's debts.

IN France, when people married a second time, especially widows who married rather too soon for local sensibilities, it was customary for neighbours to gather around the home of the couple at night and shout, whistle, hiss, groan, ring cowbells, blow horns and beat pans and kettles. The crowd would often be wearing masks and outlandish costumes. They would not stop this racket, or *charivari*, until the newly married couple purchased their peace with a ransom, usually food and drink, or money. In Germany, the *charivari* is known as *Katzenmusik* – cats' concert.

A Family Affair

IN Saudi Arabia, Vietnam and in the Himalayas, the ideal match for a girl is thought to be her mother's brother's son, while for a boy it is his father's sister's daughter.

For Richer for Poorer

WHEN Donald Trump married his longtime girlfriend Marla Maples, no one expected the wedding to be understated. Here are just some of the statistics:

1,700 guests, excluding the sixty-five security guards, 195 approved press, twenty-five approved TV crews, and eighty still photographers. Amongst the delicacies served were: seventy pounds of Beluga caviar, 10,000 shrimps, 2,000 racks of lamb, fifty pounds of beef fillet, thirty-five turkeys, 1,320 bottles of Cristal champagne.

SHEIK Rashid Bin Saeed Al Maktoum wanted his son's wedding to be a special occasion for all the family. So when Mohammed married Princess Salama in Dubai in May 1981, it cost an estimated £30 million, and lasted seven days. There were 20,000 wedding guests.

Affairs to Remember

IN Alaska, wedding parties, together with a marriage commissioner who will perform the ceremony, can be flown to the middle of a glacier for a truly white wedding. That's one way of keeping the champagne cold!

If a glacier does not appeal, there are some other unusual places to get hitched. Football fans can marry at the Aston Villa football club, where the newly-weds are allowed on to the pitch after the ceremony, and personalized scoreboard messages can be arranged.

Alternatively, for the macho man, a cave wedding can be arranged. The Dan-yr-Ogof caves in the Swansea Valley in Wales are available for underground weddings, which can take place in the appropriately named Cathedral Cave, 150 feet below the surface.

Notable Nuptials

HOLLYWOOD marriages don't always last long, but the stars seem to keep trying. Zsa Zsa Gabor, Mickey Rooney, Lana Turner and Liz Taylor have all been married eight times (at the time of going to print), Stan Laurel was married seven times. John Huston, Hedy Lamarr, Rex Harrison, Claude Rains, and Gloria Swanson all stopped at six.

ANOTHER favourite pastime of the stars is marrying people many years their junior. Charlie Chaplin was fifty-four when he married his fourth wife, who was eighteen at the time. The marriage worked, producing eight children, the last one when Chaplin was seventy-three. Groucho Marx was forty years older than his wife, Eden, and Gene Kelly was forty-one years older than his last wife. Bing Crosby was fifty when he married nineteen-year-old Kathryn, and that marriage lasted twenty-four years, until his death in 1977.

WINSTON Churchill claimed that his most brilliant achievement was to persuade his wife to marry him.

ATTILA the Hun's wife may not have had such a bad time as we might imagine – apparently Attila drank himself to death on his wedding night.

ABRAHAM Lincoln's first words to his future wife, whom he met at a dance, were: 'Miss Todd, I want to dance with you in the worst way.'

LUCREZIA Borgia was married four times before she was twenty-two.

CLEOPATRA is widely known to have been the mistress of both Caesar and Mark Antony. Less well known, however, is the fact that she was married twice – to two of her brothers.

IVAN the Terrible seemed to apply his warring principles to his love conquests. When he decided to marry, he ordered all the nobles of his realm to present their daughters of marriageable age to him in Moscow. The penalty if they refused was death. Needless to say, they all complied, and 1,500 young women arrived in Moscow where Ivan inspected them all. He was married twice, using this method of selection, and it seems he loved both his wives. When his second wife died, he saw no reason to discontinue his unusual match-making methods, and chose number three. She, however, was so devastated when she found she was chosen that she became ill and died in 1569 before the marriage was consummated.

THOMAS Edison proposed to his wife in Morse code. He began to lose his hearing when he was quite young, so he taught his wife to use Morse code while he was courting her. She responded with an excited 'Yes' – also in Morse.

ARISTOTLE was so in love with his wife, Herpyllis, that when he died, apart from leaving her homes, money and slaves, his will allowed for her to remarry to prevent her having a lonely old age. There was one provision, though. The executors must ensure that she did not remarry below her social status.

WHEN William the Conqueror met the woman of his dreams, Matilda of Flanders, he was dismayed when she refused his proposal, sent through emissaries. In fact, she stated she would rather be a nun than marry him. So William galloped off to Lille, forced his way into her chambers, grabbed Matilda by the hair, dragged her round the room, flung her to the floor, and beat her into submission. They were married soon after.

THE course of true love did not run smooth for the nineteenth-century Italian patriot Giuseppe Garibaldi. In June 1859, at the age of fifty-two, he fell madly in love with an eighteen-year-old girl, Guiseppina Raimondi. He proposed marriage, but she turned him down because she was in love with another. However, six months later, Garibaldi received an apologetic note from the girl, agreeing to marry him. He was overjoyed, and married her one month later. But, just as they were leaving the chapel after the ceremony, he was handed an anonymous note saying the girl had been forced into the marriage by her father. Garibaldi, humiliated, stormed out of the chapel, and never saw his bride again.

JANE Austen seems to have been a prankster, as she has two fake entries in the register of banns and marriages for the years 1755 to 1812 for the parish of the village of Steventon in Hampshire. They are on the page on which sample entries are provided for inexperienced clergymen, and are not amongst the lists of real people. She names a different 'husband' each time – the first is Henry Frederic Howard Fitzwilliam of London, and the second is Edmund Arthur William Mortimer of Liverpool. The bride and groom have signed themselves Jack Smith and Jane Smith, late Austen, and Jack and Jane are also the witnesses.

I Do, Etc

TING Ming Siong, from Sibu, Sarawak, in Malaysia, must be a terrific person – at least, 891 people think he's the best. That's how many times he has been best man between 1976 and 1994.

MARY Hamilton who lived as a man, was convicted on 7 October 1746 of bigamy – with fourteen wives.

THE fourth Mogul Emperor, Jahangir, who ruled from 1605 to 1627, would put the average womanizer in the shade. He had a harem of 300 wives, 5,000 more women, and 1,000 young men to provide him with variety.

GIANNI Vigliotto, aka Fred Jipp, aka Nikolai Peruskov, married 104 women – four of them aboard one ship in 1968! He was finally arrested in 1983, and sentenced to twenty-eight years for fraud, and six for bigamy.

RICHARD and Carole Roble of South Hempstead, New York, were first married in 1969. They enjoyed their wedding so much, they just kept marrying each other. So far, they have married fifty-three times.

ADRIENNE Cuyot of Belgium was engaged 652 times and married fifty-three times over a twenty-three-year period.

HAJ Ahmel, who was once Bey of Algeria, had 385 wives who all came from different parts of the world so that none of them could talk to each other about him. In fact, he created his own Tower of Bey-bel!

QUEEN Kahina of Aures, Algeria, had a harem of 400 male concubines.

MRS Theresa Vaughn, of Sheffield, was far more moral than Queen Kahina, she married her men – all sixty-one of them! She appeared before a court on 19 December 1922, accused of remarrying without first obtaining a divorce from Mr Vaughn. She confessed that since separating from her husband five years earlier, she had travelled widely through the British Isles, Germany and South Africa. Instead of collecting useless souvenirs, she had accumulated husbands – at a rate of more than one a month.

FOR several centuries it was the custom in Istanbul harems to use candles fastened to the backs of tortoises for lighting.

Rites of Spring

ANTHONY Pike and Jennifer Fairfax-Ross had an unusual courtship. They were stranded on a five-foot-long life raft for three days in the Caribbean, with no water and no food except raw seagull meat and a few raisins. They were rescued near Haiti on 23 June 1975, and married two weeks later.

IN Kanye, Botswana, villagers gathered to watch champion sprinter Marian Assa being chased by seven men. The nineteen-year-old promised to marry the man who could manage to catch her, after the list was narrowed down to the seven suitors. She was finally caught by twenty-eight-year-old Eli Bewa, a fruit trader from a local village.

It's Never Too Late

OCTAVIO Guillen and Adriana Martinez did not want to rush into marriage. So they waited until they had been engaged for sixty-seven years before marrying in June 1969 in Mexico City. They were both eighty-two.

I982 was a good year for fifty-eight-year-old Mary Cooper and sixty-year-old George Reese, who were both caretakers. They met through a radio talk show in Cincinnati called *Desperate and Dateless*, and were married on the air.

WHEN Learlene Harvey married Artis Hooker in Louisville, Kentucky, the wedding was well attended – by their eleven children, thirty-eight grandchildren, and thirty great-grandchildren from their previous marriages. At the time of their wedding Learlene was seventy-six, and Artis seventy.

HARRY Stevens went into the record books when he married eighty-four-year-old Thelma Lucas, on 3 December 1984. Harry was 103 years old, and always liked younger women.

MINNIE Munro, on the other hand, could be accused of falling for a toy boy when she married Dudley Reid at Point Clare, New South Wales, Australia. Dudley, a young lad of eighty-three, was nineteen years younger than 102-year-old Minnie.

A man of 115 who won a health contest for the elderly in northern Thailand fell in love with and subsequently planned to marry the 106-year-old woman who came in second.

Never the Twain Shall Meet . . . Again

AMONG the early Anglo-Saxons, a husband could divorce his wife for being too passionate.

DIVORCED men over fifty, if they remarry, tend to marry women who are on average four years younger; despite popular belief only one in twenty-five marries a woman twenty or more years younger than he.

EIGHTY-FIVE per cent of divorced people remarry, but only forty per cent of these second marriages survive.

IN the Malabar region of India a wife can get rid of her husband simply by leaving his shoes outside the door.

STATISTICS show that June marriages have the highest divorce rate.

TWO out of five murders in the US are either wives killing their husbands or husbands murdering their wives.

IN a survey of 9,000 American husbands who were asked if they would marry their wives again, 2,000 said they would not under any circumstances!

WHEN Eugene Schneider and his wife were divorced in 1976, there were still some hard feelings between them. So when the judge told them to divide their assets equally, Eugene did just that – he cut their New Jersey house in half with a chain saw.

THE largest divorce settlement ever was for Soraya Khash-oggi when she divorced her husband Adnan in 1982. She received £500 million, plus property.

FATHER of eleven, eighty-four-year-old Salvatore Zim-mitte, and his wife Giovanna, eighty, divorced in Naples after sixty-two years of marriage. The grounds: Incompatibility!

MONICA von Bredow is divorcing her husband because he fell in love with a dinosaur. Bernard von Bredow built the dinosaur from bones he found. He gave it skin and hair, then named it Oscar. Monica cites Oscar in the divorce petition, claiming perhaps it had become a 'saur' point in their marriage.

WHEN Robert Nordyke, a matrimonial lawyer in Salem, was looking for new offices, he was delighted to find that a bank had vacated a space which was perfect for him. Mr Nordyke was a little unsure about what to do with the drive-through banking window, with its microphone, glass, and retractable drawer. But then he came up with the perfect solution – drive-through divorce. He claims to have handled about 400 drive-through divorces – after all, it rains a lot in Oregon, and who wants to get wet just for a silly old divorce?

WHEN Johann Klaus, a sculptor, created a lifelike bust of his wife, he had no idea it would end in divorce. His wife, Annie, was furious that he showed her to be enormously fat, with a double chin. Annie claimed he should have made it 'as he sees me in his heart'. Ex-husband Johann said, 'I did, gigantically fat with that double chin.'

Let Them Eat Cake

IN medieval England, each guest brought a bun or small cake to the wedding. These sweets were piled on top of each other, and the bride and groom kissed over the stack to ensure many healthy children.

IN Bermuda, the bride's cake is a tiered fruitcake, covered with silver leaf and topped with a tiny cedar tree. The tree is then planted by the bride and groom. The groom also has a cake, which is a plain sponge.

WHEN Roseanne Barr married Tom Arnold in February 1990, it was to be expected that the two 'foodies' would have a pretty spectacular wedding cake – and they didn't disappoint the watching guests. The first layer was chocolate with a Bavarian cream filling and was covered with white chocolate icing. The second and third layers were of carrot cake with cream cheese and apricot icing. White orchids decorated the cake, and elaborate latticework covered the sides. Whilst guests waited hungrily for them to cut the cake and pass round a few slices, the bride and groom had a different idea. They cut the cake, and started feeding each other. By the time they had finished, they had eaten two layers themselves. Their faces, hair and clothes were covered in cake and icing.

THE first designed tiered wedding cake was originally modelled on the church of St Brides in Fleet Street.

QUEEN Victoria's wedding cake was three yards wide and weighed 300 pounds. In 1974, Christie's, the auction house, sold an uneaten portion of this cake for £100.

THE French have traditionally thrown wheat at the bridal couple, Sicilians throw wheat bread and salt, while the English, in the past, threw pieces of cake. All are symbols of fertility. In some parts of England, rather than tossing cake at the couple, bridal guests ensured their fertility by smashing a plate of salt over the groom's head.

Words of Warning

'I've only slept with men I've been married to.'

Elizabeth Taylor

'The outcome of a successful marriage depends on the income.'

Groucho Marx

'There is only one thing that keeps me from being a happily married woman – him.'

Lana Turner

'Marriage is an alliance entered into by a man who can't sleep with the window shut, and a woman who can't sleep with the window open.'

George Bernard Shaw

'By all means marry; if you get a good wife, you'll be happy. If you get a bad one, you'll become a philosopher.'

Socrates

'People who haven't spoken to each other for years are on speaking terms again today – including the bride and groom.'

Dorothy Parker, when she married Alan Campbell for the second time

'Marriage is a great institution, but I'm not ready for an institution.'

Mae West

Nippon Nuptials

TWO out of five Japanese marriages are still arranged by go-betweens.

IN Japan, a family will sometimes hire a private detective to make sure there is no embarrassing skeleton in the cupboard of the intended's family, before a marriage takes place.

JAPANESE women are shunning traditional weddings in favour of more personal ceremonies. Their choice of venue, however, may seem a little strange. One of the most popular venues for the trendy Japanese wedding is the handbag department of the Mitsushi department store in Tokyo. The bride can be sure she's really bagged her man!

IN case you have ever wondered whether the inscrutable Japanese are really a romantic nation, this may help to enlighten you. The Japanese language has more words for rice than for love.

AHIT series of articles in the Japanese magazine *Spa* is called 'Look for a Tokyo Girl with a House'. There is one article per issue and it shows photographs of a single woman, lists her hobbies, blood type, taste in men – and the value of the estate she expects to inherit.

IN the 20-30 age group in Japan, there are 9.3 million men and 9 million women, so the women can afford to be choosy. This has inspired a new business – consultants who teach men how to talk to women, how to dress, and how to be a considerate husband.

OF the 80,000 couples who marry each year in Japan, more than 20,000 now take their vows abroad, due to the extraordinarily high cost of weddings in Japan. A typical wedding can cost up to 4 million yen, (£25,000) and usually includes four changes of clothing for the bride (two kimonos, a Western-style white wedding dress and a going-away outfit).

Bewitched

AS protection against the evil eye, Moroccan brides have to keep their eyes tightly closed throughout the wedding ceremony.

FILIPINO folklore dictates that the bride and her wedding party all dress in the same colour so that the bride blends in with her attendants thus preventing evil spirits identifying her and stealing her away before the wedding.

ONE pretty distasteful old English custom was for a young girl to prick an orange all over with a needle and sleep with it under her arm. The next day she would persuade her beloved to eat it, and that would ensure her conquest. Perhaps it made her seem ap-peeling!

IN ancient Rome, a bride would rub the door post of her new home with grease to erase any evil.

IN India, to protect newlyweds from evil spirits, each was symbolically married to a tree during the wedding ceremony.

Weddings from Hell

IN 1981 Paulo Cesa Bonfim was so delighted when his fiancée recovered from a paralysing disease, he walked halfway across Brazil carrying a large cross on his back to give thanks to God. When he returned, he found his fiancée had married another man.

DEBORAH Yager had a call from her priest one week before her December 1993 wedding – he'd double-booked the church, so the time of the ceremony would have to be changed – he could sandwich her between another wedding and a mass. Deborah was not happy. She thought this was a bad omen. It was.

On the wedding day, her sister – the maid of honour – dislocated her shoulder getting out of a car and was in such pain throughout the ceremony she could barely hold the bouquet. The priest, nervous that the wedding might run overtime, skipped an entire section of the ceremony, then forgot the groom's name. Gregory, the groom, was so furious that when he opened his mouth to recite his vows, he said, 'I Deborah, take you, Gregory.'

The reception went perfectly. The happy (and greatly relieved) couple flew to their skiing honeymoon in the French Alps. On the second day Deborah catapulted onto a nine-foot stretch of rocks, broke her kneecap, and had to be carried down the mountain on a stretcher. At the hospital she was told she needed surgery. The doctor failed to give her an adequate anaesthetic, and she felt the entire operation. Two weeks after returning home, Gregory slipped and fell on a patch of ice, and needed ten stitches in a head cut. Two weeks after that, their car was stolen. Perhaps their wedding vows should have been: 'For better for worse, and worse, and worse . . .'

WHEN Thomas and Martha Scearce planned their wedding at the Episcopal church in Danville, Virginia, they were delighted to hear that they were to be married by the appropriately named Reverend Dewey Loving. They felt this romantic-sounding name augured well for their future happiness. However, their joy turned to horror when, in the middle of the ceremony, Reverend Loving fell down dead.

MARIE Holley decided that traditional floral centre-pieces were just too ordinary for her – she put a pretty little bowl of goldfish swimming in coloured water in the middle of each of the ten tables. Everyone thought this was delightfully innovative – until the goldfish began dying and floating to the top of the bowls during dinner. It appears Marie had put a little too much colouring in the water, and the fish just could not survive.

The Dating Game

IN Singapore, the government gets involved in matchmaking. One government agency helps to pair off college graduates, while another one works for those lacking higher education.

MRS Jared Bates, who was widowed in 1800, was clearly ahead of her time when it came to Lonely Hearts advertising. On her husband's tombstone, after the usual RIP, she had inscribed: 'His widow, Aged 24, who mourns as one who can be comforted, lives at 7 Elm Street this village and possesses every qualification for a Good Wife.'

J WINGO International may be one of the most expensive dating agencies in the world with fees of up to $125,000. One client demanded a man who earned over $250,000 per annum, lived no more than ten minutes from her house, and had erections of over seven inches. She was shown the door. After all, even if they could provide her with the first two conditions, no one was prepared to get out the tape measure to satisfy the third!

RESEARCHERS at Yale University came up with some pretty discouraging figures for unmarried women: A woman born in the mid-fifties who is still single at thirty had only a twenty per cent chance of getting married. Worse still, an unmarried forty-year-old woman has more chance of being killed by a terrorist than of tying the knot.

SINGLE men living in Alaska have trouble finding mates – so they advertise in a magazine called *Alaskan Men*, which lists available men for women who are hunting for a husband.

The town of Talkeetna is typical – a lot of snow, bears and moose, a few trees, but no women. In fact, the bachelors there have formed a society. In December, they invite women from all over the USA to come and meet them. Then they have a contest where women have to go through an obstacle course, carrying water and chopping ice to win a prize for being 'Wilderness Woman of the Year'.

RICH Gosse is the founder of American Singles, and organizes singles conventions. For $30 per day, customers get one and a half days of workshops, plus a series of love games, and a Saturday night dance. During the conventions, there are people selling booklets on how to answer the personal ads, therapists taking everyone back to happy childhood memories, and lessons on how to become a yogi and how to improve your self-esteem.

Connect for Singles offers a free trial membership, and badges bearing slogans such as 'Dating is like a snowstorm – you have to suffer through a lot of flakes'.

SINGLE women flocked to the town of Herman, Minneapolis, after Dan Ellison made a speech for the town business association, lamenting that so many women had fled the rural hamlet for city jobs. Left behind were seventy-eight bachelors, competing for the town's ten single women. Before long, three bachelors had married and more than twenty single women had moved into the area. Busloads of single women arrived for day trips – and before long, Dan found himself one of the few bachelors left in town.

The story ends happily, however, because he eventually met Gwen Fredrickson, who decided to move to Herman after reading the stories in the press. She claims she just wanted to enjoy a quiet life with her son, Bobby, and was not thinking of the town's eligible men.

THERE is a leafy park, just west of Tiananmen Square in Beijing, which is known as 'Love Corner'. On Fridays and Sundays, hundreds of lonely hearts flock to the park in the hope of meeting their future partners. There are more than 200,000 singles aged between twenty-five and thirty-five in Beijing, and many have failed to find a partner through the usual avenues of friends, work, relatives, or matchmakers. Marriage remains mandatory, but dance halls and discos are very expensive, and sometimes quite inaccessible. So – off they go to Love Corner, where the usual approach is a brief discussion about the weather. According to one hopeful twenty-nine-year-old woman: 'We talk, and if it's not working I say, 'Sorry, we don't seem to match.' And she moves onto the next.

AMERICAN women need go no further than their own homes to find the man of their dreams. The latest way of meeting Mr Right is by *male* order! The catalogue, called the Bachelor Book, is packed with eligible men.

IN New England, large ladies have their own singles places. The Well Rounded Club invites big beautiful women and the men who prefer them to join in their dances.

INCURABLE Romantix is a service for computer users who need help with their love bytes. For $35 a year, subscribers to this New York City based service receive one letter each month, which they sign before sending on to their lover. In the letter, they replace F3 with the name of the beloved, and F4 with that of the subscriber. One such letter reads: 'Love is a strange thing F3. You cannot chase it, you cannot pursue it, you cannot manufacture it. But when it happens, as in the great romance we two now have, F3 and F4, it becomes a treasure that no treasure chest could ever hold . . . I am yours this Valentine's Day, F3 . . . Forever, F4.'

Food of Love

IN preparation for a wedding in Crete two loaves of bread are baked, decorated with flowers, tied together with white ribbon and separated by a bottle of wine. The ribbon is cut when the couple enter the church.

AT Chinese weddings, the bride and groom drink from goblets of wine and honey, tied together with a red string.

YOUNG Irishmen used to race from the church to the bride's house for a bottle of ale. The groom always poured the last drops for good fortune.

UNTIL recently, bear's nose was a delicacy often served at Chinese wedding feasts.

AN old French custom involved a loaf of bread. The bride's father would lay a long loaf of bread in the marriage bed to ensure the bride's fertility and the groom's virility. The condition of the bread the next morning signified the success or failure of the wedding night.

IN Peru, the marriage bed is decorated with red and green chilli peppers to assure the bridal couple a fruitful and passionate marriage. Not to mention a pretty hot night!

THE custom of toasting the newlyweds is believed to have originated in sixteenth-century France, where lavish feasts were popular. A man drank to the health of the bride and then placed a piece of bread at the bottom of the wine goblet and passed the cup to each guest. The bride, last to receive the cup, ate the wine-soaked toast and received everyone's best wishes.

AT a Greek wedding, sugar-coated almonds are served. They are symbolic, in that the fresh almond has a bitter-sweet taste that is symbolic of life itself. The sugar coating is added with the hope that the life of the new family has more sweetness than bitterness. They are always served in odd numbers because an odd number is indivisible, just as the newlyweds should remain undivided.

THE largest item on any menu in the world is probably roasted camel, which is sometimes served at Bedouin wedding feasts. The camel is stuffed with a sheep's carcass, which is stuffed with chickens, which are stuffed with fish, which are stuffed with eggs. The groom probably spends the evening hoping his new mother-in-law doesn't get the hump!

Bottom Drawer

THE word 'trousseau' comes from the French word *trousse*, meaning bundle. It originally described the bundle of belongings the bride carried with her to her new home.

A MODERATE trousseau for an 1897 bride was suggested by The *Ladies' Home Journal* as: 'Six new pieces of each kind of underwear, three new pairs of stays, one nice pair of walking shoes, one pair of heavy boots, a pair of dress slippers, a pair of bedroom slippers, a pair of low patent leather shoes, and a pair of low russet shoes will be required. As to stockings, six pairs, either of lisle or cotton, with the one silk pair to wear with your wedding gown. A dozen new handkerchiefs, having narrow hemstitched borders with the initials of your maiden name in white letters in the corner of each . . .'

Advice is also given concerning the number of dresses, which is concluded: '. . . but do not make the mistake so often made, of buying clothes that aren't suited to your position in life.'

The Blushing Bride

To the early Hawaiians, a lady who weighed 300 pounds was approaching perfection.

In India brides traditionally dress like a gilded rose – in a sari of pink or red trimmed with gold.

The world's longest wedding dress train was made in Germany in 1992 and measured 515 feet.

Customary colours for brides: black in Spain, red in China and Islamic cultures, white in Japan, blue in Russia where it is considered a symbol of purity. In Korea brides wear bright reds and yellows although yellow is frowned upon by most cultures because it is considered a sign of a wife's intention to cheat on her husband.

Until recently, Icelandic brides wore black velvet wedding dresses embroidered with silver and gold.

If a girl wanted to indicate her virginity in Tudor England, she exposed her bosom! However, she would modestly wear full sleeves which covered her arms to the wrists.

WHEN Mary Queen of Scots married Francis, Dauphin of France, she scandalized the wedding guests by wearing her favourite colour – white. White was the traditional colour of mourning in France, and was considered unlucky.

IN early Saxon days and through the eighteenth century, it was the poorer bride who came to her wedding dressed in a plain white robe. This was in the nature of a public statement that she brought nothing with her to her marriage and that therefore her husband was not responsible for her debts.

NELLIE Custis was the first American woman to wear a long, white veil of lace when she married Major Lawrence Lewis, an aide to President Washington. Nellie chose lace because the major had once glimpsed her face through the lace curtains of an open window, and afterwards he couldn't stop telling her how beautiful she had looked.

IT was once customary for Finnish brides to cut their hair short on their wedding day and then never show it again.

IN Sweden, chives, garlic or rosemary were put into the bride's bouquet to stop dwarves from bothering her on her wedding day. In Poland, it was believed that sprinkling the bride's bouquet with sugar would keep her sweet-tempered.

IN fourteenth-century France, the wedding guests rushed for the bride's garter (which symbolized the release of the virgin girdle) because it bestowed great luck. But because people were often hurt in the rush, brides began to remove their garters and throw them to the crowd instead.

You Are Cordially Invited . . .
─────────

I N 1982, in New York's Yankee Stadium, the Reverend Sun Myung Moon married 2,075 couples, many of them complete strangers to their new spouses. The record-breaking walk up the aisle was watched by thousands of witnesses.

M ICHAEL Ince and Lorraine Kraemer were married in a plane, then parachuted, along with their wedding party, to their reception near Wellsville, Kansas, on 16 June 1984. A week later, Cynthia Harrington and Chris Penny went one better. They leapt out of a plane somewhere over Illinois and exchanged vows on the way down.

C OURTNEY and Cozy Platt made it legal in a submarine.

V ICTOR and Deborah Radeka marched down the aisle of the supermarket where they met.

W HEN Bruce Laker married Vanda Yong on the Isle of Wight, they were more traditional. A beautiful white gown was purchased, as was an elegant black dinner jacket. Except, Bruce wore the dress and Vanda wore the trousers. They decided that as Vanda was planning to be the breadwinner of the family, and Bruce was going to stay home and mind the children, they might as well start out as they meant to continue – as role swappers.

TERRY Schladwiler and Natalie Lester were married during the World's Fair in New Orleans – dangling from a cable in a gondola some 170 feet over the Mississippi River. Two days later, Jim Kovatch and his bride Nora Harris pledged their troth atop the fair's twenty-storey Ferris Wheel.

THE Reverend Charlotte Richards owns five chapels, and has married half a million people in thirty-four years. These are not conventional weddings, however. They are drive-in weddings in Las Vegas. The ceremony takes about ten minutes – unless it is Valentine's Day, in which case it lasts about five minutes. One Valentine's Day she managed to marry 147 couples in twenty-four hours. Many of the happy couples don't even bother to turn off the engine or undo their seat belts for the occasion. They just drive up, make their vows, and drive off. Some people still do it in style though, arriving in limousines, or on bicycles, or even roller skates.

US National Aerobics champion Debbie Teresi, thirty-four, wanted something special when she married her coach, Joseph Wenson, in July 1994. They staged the world's first aerobics wedding at a San Francisco shopping mall. Wearing a white leotard with a detachable train and entering to the beat of dance music, the bride was escorted down the escalator by her father, watched by more than 1,000 guests and passing shoppers. The twelve members of the wedding party wore shorts and leotards. The vows reflected the theme – she promised to join him for Monday night football, he vowed to watch aerobics videos with her.

W HEN Tony Perkins and Berinthia Berenson married in 1973, the best man at their Cape Cod wedding was Murray – Tony's pet collie.

J ANNENE Swift of Los Angeles was a real sucker for the strong silent type. So when she finally walked up the aisle in Lafayette Park in 1976, her groom was the perfect partner – a fifty-pound pet rock.

Of Mice and Men

D ISNEY fanatics Fay Cramp and Mel Roseman dressed formally for their Florida wedding on 19 December 1993. The bride wore a beautiful traditional gown in white satin, and the groom wore a white tuxedo. However, her stockings and his cummerbund and socks were a little less traditional. They bore images of Mickey Mouse. That was just the beginning of their Mickey Mouse Wedding. Seventy guests were greeted by a fourteen-piece brass band playing the Mickey Mouse Club anthem. Mingling among the guests were Mickey and Minnie Mouse, Goofy, Pluto, Donald Duck, Roger Rabbit and the chipmunks Chip 'n' Dale. They performed three song and dance productions. Four guests were on stilts. The bride was accompanied down the aisle by the strains of 'When You Wish upon a Star'. After the ceremony, everyone wore mouse ears. The finale of the cabaret was the cast singing 'Zip-a-Dee-Doo-Dah', fireworks erupting from the ceiling and from the hands of a ten-foot inflated Mickey. At the same time, a cannon sprayed a thick coating of confetti all over the room.

DONNA Krumm, of California, wanted to marry on 4 July, but could not find a judge or a priest who was free on that day – so her best friend answered an ad in a magazine placed by the Universal Life Church, sending a cheque for five dollars to become an ordained minister, and married them herself!

ONE of the most unusual brides wore white, with a delicate little veil. She seemed a little overweight, but then she was pregnant. Although 6,000 pounds is a lot for any bride to weigh. Bonnie and Shorty, two white rhinos, married in Bayou Wildlife Park in Dickinson, Iowa at a wedding officiated over by Justice of the Peace, Mike Nelson. The zookeepers had decided that Bonnie's baby should be born within wedlock.

Alone at Last

IN the Eskimo tradition it is customary for the bridesmaids and the bride to warm the bed for the groom. He may decide how many of the bridesmaids will remain in the bed during the marriage consummation.

AMONG the Bantu Kavironda tribes, the bride and groom must consummate their marriage before a large group of young girls and women. This is to show publicly that the marriage is legal – it is believed the women will spread the word more quickly than men. The husband's prowess and virility, along with the success of the consummation, are measured by the amount of giggling and embarrassment the witnesses express.

IN Algeria, the bridegroom throws eggs at his bride during their marriage consummation. The pelting ensures her fertility and easy childbirth.

TRADITIONALLY in Sweden the bride would go through the entire wedding ceremony with her shoes untied, then proceed to her honeymoon chamber, go to bed and consummate her marriage, still wearing the untied shoes. She would sleep with the shoes dangling on her feet, hoping that they would fall off by themselves during the night, an indication that she would bear children as easily as she removed her shoes.

THE term honeymoon, referring to the time period when the marriage consummation takes place, derives from the ancient Northern European tradition of drinking honeyed wine as an aphrodisiac during the first month of marriage.

Taking No Chance on Love

ONE Louisiana man included a 'coitus clause' in his prenuptial agreement. His future wife agreed that she limit her sexual demands on him to once a week. When she later demanded sex up to three times a day, he claimed she had broken the agreement and was therefore not entitled to maintenance. The court ruled in favour of the wife, as 'the fault here alleged by the husband is not in law any fault'. Other premarital agreements have tried to stipulate that the wife should not increase her weight by more than ten pounds above her bridal night weight, and that belching and flatulence are in breach of contract.

W HEN Rex and Teresa LeGalley decided to marry, their prenuptial agreement went even further than most. Admitting they were both 'detail people', on 5 July 1995 they filed a sixteen-page document as a public record in the county clerk's office which included the following agreements:

* To engage in healthy sex three to five times per week
* To retire for the night at 11.30 p.m. and awake at 6.30
* To assign Rex full responsibility for family leadership and decision making
* To live within a budget and pay cash for everything unless agreed to otherwise
* To never drive any closer to another car than one car length per ten m.p.h. and never allow their fuel gauges to drop below the half-tank mark

Whatever happened to spontaneity?

E VEN the arranging of a premarital agreement has become an important part of the American marriage scene. A book of wedding planning issued by Tiffany's suggests the appropriate form for such a meeting should be 'A small lunch for four, i.e. the couple and their respective lawyers'.

For anyone having second thoughts before the big day, Californians can go into therapy before they marry. A Los Angeles marriage and family therapist offers bridal support groups and premarital counselling.

Gay Weddings

During the Roman Empire, male soldiers were often married to each other prior to battle.

133 North American tribes, including the Navajo, Mojave, Lakota, Eskimo, Yuma, Klamath, Crow, and Blackfoot, commonly accepted alternative gender roles, including same-sex marriages.

Between 1368 and 1644, during the Ming dynasty, a form of male marriage developed in China's Fujian province. A younger man moved into the household of an older 'adoptive brother' whose parents treated him as a son-in-law. Many of these marriages lasted for more than twenty years.

In nineteenth-century China, the exclusively female Golden Orchid Associations were common in the Guangzhou province. Within these groups, lesbian couples could marry. After exchanging ritual gifts, the couple would hold a wedding feast, and later were allowed to adopt young girls.

On 24 April 1993 – the day before the second massive gay and lesbian march on Washington – 'the Wedding' took place on the steps of the IRS building. More than 2,000 couples were united in the ceremony.

Love Hurts

Cupid's arrows can hit anyone, anytime. But it was a sad day for twenty-year-old George when he fell in love. The object of George's desires was young and shapely but – it was an Austin Metro car! Reported in 1992 in 'Sexual and Marital Therapy', it was the first case of this rare fetish to be studied in Britain. George also liked the Vauxhall Nova, the Fiat Uno and the Ford Fiesta, but most of all he loved his Metro. He would drive for hours looking for spots he could be alone with his car. A psychiatrist who was called in to help poor, lovelorn George said he was so attached to his car that he showed no interest in women, and only became sexually aroused when he looked at his Metro. After months of reconditioning, George's preferences have changed for the more ordinary, the opposite sex. Perhaps one day he will find a wife named Mercedes.

Rings on Her Fingers

The engagement ring originated with the practice of purchasing a bride. The ring represented part of the groom's payment for his loved one.

UNTIL 1215, the bride only received one ring – upon her engagement. Then the Pope declared a longer waiting period between betrothal and the marriage, so a second ring, the wedding ring, was placed on the bride's finger when she finally married.

DIAMONDS were first used in engagement rings in medieval Italy – their durability symbolizing enduring love.

IN the days of Queen Elizabeth I, the wedding ring was worn on the thumb of the right hand.

THE average diamond size for an engagement ring is three quarters of a carat but New York jewellers, Hammerman Brothers, recently provided an anonymous client with an engagement ring for his beloved bearing a fifty-two carat emerald-cut diamond as its centrepiece. The two side stones were a mere three and a half carats each.

THE Hindus associated rubies with fire, believing they radiated heat, so the gems became popular set in engagement rings.

THERE was a superstition that if a man gave his lover an emerald ring, the stone would shatter if the relationship broke up.

WHEN choosing that simple wedding band, remember that it takes more than two tons of South African rock to produce less than one ounce of gold, and miners have dug as deep as two and a half miles underground to obtain that ounce of precious metal.

IN ancient Egypt, wedding rings were originally made of rushes or hemp and were replaced annually. Later, before coins were minted, gold rings were used as currency. As a token of his trust, the Egyptian husband would give his wife one of these rings, placing it on the third finger of her left hand, since it was believed that love travelled through a vein in that finger directly to the heart.

Groomed for Success

AN 1891 bridal journal commented: 'The lack of beauty and daintiness about the average man is never so fully realized as when it is seen of how little importance he is at a wedding. Of course, he is a necessity but he is not a picturesque one; whether the ceremony takes place during the day or at night, he is never anything more than a mere dark blotch upon it.'

By 1905, however, the groom was considered important enough to merit a little advice of his own concerning his role and his wardrobe. He was told by *The Ladies' Home Journal*: 'Beyond the wedding clothes, an elaborate outfit for a man is not in good taste. Overhaul your wardrobe and supply or renew what is needed.' Advice is also given for the groom to '. . . request the ushers not to push the fun so far as to resemble friendly persecution. The rice, violently thrown, has caused much trouble. A recent bride was made permanently deaf from a grain of rice entering her ear.'

Flower Power

THE tossing of the bridal bouquet originated with the ancient Romans. It was their custom to light the first lamp in a couple's new home with a torch and then toss the torch to the wedding party. In the fourteenth century, the French substituted a bouquet for the torch and added that whoever caught the bouquet would be wed next.

IN the late 1800s an American bride sometimes carried as many small bouquets as she had bridesmaids. The bouquets were tied together, one of them concealing a ring. When the bride and groom were ready to leave, the room was darkened, the bride throwing the bouquets to the guests. Whoever caught the bouquet with the ring inside was thought to be the next to be married.

Government and Love

IN the eighteenth century, the Mayor of Amberg, in Germany, decided to restrict marriage to the landed gentry. Not unsurprisingly, this included the mayor and his friends and excluded almost everyone else in the town. In order to obtain a marriage licence a couple had to prove they owned property, creating an insurmountable obstacle for penniless young lovers.

The owner of the home at Number 8 Seminargasse took pity on the town's landless lovebirds and agreed to sell them his house for a low price, qualifying them as landowners so they could marry. Less the romantic than the opportunist, the owner would buy the house back the next day for less than he sold it the previous day, thus ensuring the marriage for the couple and a profit for himself.

Since that time, Number 8 Seminargasse has been sold and re-purchased thousands of times, more than any other house in the world. Although the law has been repealed the tradition continues, and Number 8 Seminargasse with its single bedroom also qualifies today as the smallest honeymoon hotel in the world.

THE National Science Foundation in America spent $84,000 studying why people fall in love.

IN Sparta, celibacy was a crime. The state designated the appropriate age for marriage – thirty for men, twenty for women. Men who remained bachelors after the age of thirty lost their right to vote, and were forbidden to attend any of the processions in which the men and women danced and revelled in the nude. Possibly in a bid to make up for this, the government would frequently order these ageing singles to parade naked in front of their fellow citizens, while singing a song in which they proclaimed themselves justly punished for having broken the marriage laws.

KUWAIT'S Charity Committee for the Marriage Project has urged married men to take up to the Islamic legal limit of four wives in order to deal with the problem of spinsterhood. To tempt men into these marriages, the charity offered up to £2,000 in loans, cheap kitchenware, and free furniture.

IT seems that the path of true love has never run smoothly – so much so that in medieval England, there were Courts of Love, presided over by Eleanor of Aquitaine, Queen of England. Problems were brought before her and a jury of great ladies, and they rendered judicial decisions. One question raised was: Is connubial love possible? The verdict of these wise ladies? A resounding No. No wonder Henry II kept Eleanor locked up in Aquitaine, while he frolicked in England.

Forsaking All Others

IN legal terms, adultery is occasionally known as 'criminal conversation'.

AN Iranian husband has the right to kill his wife if he finds her with another man.

WHEN Peter the Great found out that his wife had a lover, he had him executed and his head was put in a jar of alcohol. He presented the gruesome gift to his wife, and insisted she keep it in her bedroom.

WHEN George I was crowned King of England in 1714, his wife did not become queen because she had committed adultery. George had arrived in England from Hanover accompanied by his two mistresses – but adultery was only considered a crime if committed by a woman.

Good, Old Fashioned Advice

1816 agony aunts felt that hair was an important factor in the success or failure of a relationship. An 1816 treatise on dark hair stated:

'If the hair is very black, short and curly, the man will be given to liquor, somewhat quarrelsome, of an unsettled temper, amorous, and unsteady in his undertakings, though ardent at the beginning of the enterprise. He will be very desirous of riches but in general miss his aim, and he will be subject to much discontent. The same may be said of a woman.'

THE Victorians had some novel ideas about love and marriage. Here are some examples from almanacs of the time:

1853: The Perfect Husband:
A man what is careful of his clothes, don't drink spirits, can read the Bible without spelling out the words, and can eat a cold dinner on wash-day.

1877: How to make your Husband Happy:
Try to do not only what your husband wishes in household matters but also when and how he wishes.

Do not neglect neatness of person and surroundings.

Never speak slightingly or bitterly of or to your husband, especially in the presence of other people.

Speak gently always, and do not allow your voice to become loud and sharp. Control of the voice helps to control the temper.

How to make your Wife Happy:
Treat your wife as politely and kindly as when you were wooing her.

If your dinner does not suit you, do not spoil her appetite by scolding her about it at the time, but give whatever suggestions are needed after dinner.

Share your pleasures and your cares with her and show that you value her society and her advice.

Do not speak lightly of her cares and fatigues, but sympathize with her troubles, whether small or great.

Try to gratify her fancies, such as a flower garden or conveniences about her work. She will be reminded of your consideration or neglect many times every day by these little things.

Never Look a Gift Horse in the Mouth

THE Surma women of Ethiopia stretch their lower lips with plates in order to get a substantial 'bride price'. It seems that the larger the lip, the bigger the price paid by the amorous suitor. A small hole is pierced in a Surma girl's lower lip when she is about twenty years old. A tiny disc is then inserted, and gradually substituted with larger and larger plates until the ideal size is reached. The women do remove the plates to eat and chat, but a quiet little smooch in the back row of the cinema would probably be out of the question.

IN the US, bridal showers are customary. They are actually a Dutch custom, and are said to have begun when a Dutch maiden fell in love with a poor miller. Her father so disapproved of the match that he refused to give her a dowry. The miller's friends, who thoroughly approved of the union, then 'showered' her with gifts so she could start her new home.

IN some societies, a bride must be bought from her father. The 'bride price' varies from country to country. In Ethiopia the price may be as much as fifty cattle, a Murle groom in Southern Sudan could expect to pay forty head of cattle, a middle-class Sri Lankan will pay around £7,500 in cash.

THE price of brides in the United Arab Emirates has increased to approximately £35,000. The men have begun to object, so there is now a growing trend in imported wives!

THE cost of dowries paid by the bride's father also varies enormously around the world. A Japanese bride may be expected to bring with her the complete furnishings for a new home, in South America or the Middle East the dowry might include such practical items as jewellery, a fridge, a video recorder, or an air conditioner. Fathers with fewer funds available should try marrying off their daughters in Papua New Guinea, where yams are often the dowry.

The dowry is often considered a good thing for the woman, because if she has brought plenty of goodies with her, her husband will think twice about leaving her – if the marriage fails the bride's dowry reverts to her, and if a bride price has been paid, the bride keeps that too, thus the groom knows that if he casts aside his wife, he loses either the dowry, or the cattle he has paid for his bride.

THE Babylonians had an interesting method of ensuring that every girl had a chance of marriage, no matter how minimal her physical charms. An annual auction was held, at which the men bid for the most attractive girls. The money raised provided a dowry for the ugly girls, for whom no one would bid, so they could still find husbands.

A Kiss Is Just a Kiss

THE earth may move when sex is great, but the heart actually beats faster during a brisk walk or a heated argument.

LOVERS might not be so keen to kiss if they really knew what they were doing. When those two sets of lips meet, they are passing between them 250 types of bacteria and virus, 9 mg of water, 0.711 mg of fats, 0.7 mg of albumen and 0.18 mg of other unspecified organic matter.

PEOPLE from the Philippines have a unique way of kissing each other – they put their lips to each other's face and inhale very quickly.

Statistics

RESEARCHERS in the US have discovered that if a marriage survives the first year, the next most difficult years are the fifth and ninth. It seems the seven-year itch is a myth.

STATISTICS show that married people live longer than those who remain single. On average, a married man lives six years seven months longer than the average confirmed bachelor.

MOST women who play harps are married to men who play violins.

HALF of the married female lawyers are married to lawyers.

IN 1890, the average age of a man at his first marriage was twenty-six, and women twenty-two. Now, the ages for the first marriage are twenty-three and twenty-one.

ONE out of every three women breaks two or more engagements before they finally marry.

DISPATCHES

Mummy Dearest

THE word 'mummy' comes from the Persian word for bitumen – *moumia*. The earliest examples of mummies appear to have been soaked in a glassy, black pitch-like substance.

Around the twelfth century, mummies were used as medicine. Egyptian corpses which had been buried in sand and dried naturally were considered the least useful, so the bodies were just ground into powder to treat upset stomachs. Properly prepared mummies were imported into Europe by the ton. They were boiled and the melted oils were skimmed off to be used as ointments to stop bruising. Trade in mummies became so brisk, and prices became so inflated, that Egyptians decided to increase the supply by making copies. The mummy trade came to a grinding halt in at least one market when in 1564, Guy de la Fontaine, physician to the King of Navarre, was taken to a ship in Alexandria, where he was shown piles of mummies. He was assured by the proud salesman that none of the bodies was more than four years old.

THE mayor of San Bernado, near Bogotá in the foothills of the Andes, has decided to profit from the fact that its townsfolk mummify naturally in their coffins, rather than crumble to dust. He is building a museum where the best preserved mummies will be displayed.

THERE is a tribe in Papua New Guinea who smoke their dead. The dead citizens of Kokoa village are smoke-cured for several months, and are then carried up to a rocky outcrop where they sit with their knees drawn up to their chests, held above ground by a row of open baskets propped up on poles.

IN 1983, a graveyard was found by building workers at the village of Arica, on the edge of the Atacama Desert in South America. It contained the mummified bodies of Chinciro Indians who lived and died about 10,000 years ago – 7,000 years before the Egyptians who were famous for their mumm-ies. These mummies were preserved by skinning the body, then leaving the skin out in the sun to dry before curing it over a fire. Meanwhile, the cleaned skeleton was used as a framework to which mud or shells were attached. The skin would then be sewn back on. If the skin did not fit exactly, it would be patched with any convenient skin from animals or birds. Finally, a mask was placed over the skull, the body painted to make it look lifelike – and thus it remained for several thousand years.

Fatal Statistics

DURING the time of William Shakespeare, the infant mor-tality rate was so high that for a while the statistical average life-span was six years.

ACCORDING to a study made by the University of East Anglia, Norwich people are forty-three times more likely to die falling out of bed than they are to win the National Lottery jackpot.

MALE life expectancy in Ethiopia and Sierra Leone is the lowest in the world – 39.4 years. Japan, at 76.1 years, has the longest.

SUICIDES and conceptions both peak in the spring.

Heads You Lose . . .

WHEN Queen Austrichildia fell ill with dysentery in 580 AD, she had no confidence in the skill of her doctors. She felt they were not trying hard enough to cure her, so she made her husband, the Frankish King Guntram, promise to kill them on her grave if she died. Sadly, the queen did die and her two doctors were executed on her grave in the presence of the other court doctors.

IN nineteenth-century Britain, accounts of murders were sometimes bound in the skin of the executed killer. One such volume can be found in the Bristol Public Record Office – it dates from 1821 and contains the account of the dissection of John Horwood, together with the transcript of Horwood's trial.

THERE was a tradition in ancient Siam that royal blood should not be spilled on the ground. So, in 1688, when the King of Siam decided to execute a troublesome family member, he had him placed in a large mortar and pounded to death with a pestle. Kublai Khan had the same problem when he had to dispose of his uncle Nyan, so he had him put in a carpet and tossed backwards and forwards until he died. Presumably they didn't use the gallows because they didn't want their relatives just hanging around.

WHEN Henry VIII legalized execution by boiling in 1531, the first person to be executed by the method was a cook. Richard Roose, chef of the Bishop of Rochester, was convicted of attempting to poison the Bishop's household with hemlock, and sentenced to boiling.

THE first rope used to hang the famous pirate Captain Kidd broke. It would have been easy to escape but the Captain was too inebriated to run and was hanged as soon as a new noose could be made.

THE first, last and only portrait of the Duke of Monmouth was painted when he was dead. The Duke was executed in 1685 after leading a rebellion against his uncle James II; but it was only after he was dead that it was realized that no portrait of him existed. His head was hastily stitched back onto his body so that the portrait that now hangs in the National Gallery could be painted.

THE guillotine, the famous machine of death of the French Revolution, was invented by Dr Joseph Ignace Guillotin as a means of reducing the suffering of the condemned. It was said that the objection of Guillotine, a physician who also designed surgical instruments, to the wheel, the rack, the pincers, and the clumsy use of the sword for beheading, stemmed from the events surrounding his birth. His pregnant mother had passed a place where a criminal was being tortured on the wheel and was so distressed by his agony that she went into labour, and Joseph was born the next day.

... Tails You Win

AVA Gardner bequeathed a trust fund worth millions to her dog, Morgan, who was left her Hollywood mansion with his own personal maid until he died.

AMERICANS love their dogs every bit as much as the British – perhaps even more so, judging by the range of services offered to bereaved pet owners. At the Los Angeles Pet Memorial Park, where all customers are entitled to a full-blown funeral complete with coffin, flowers and free bereavement counselling, more than 25,000 furry, feathered, or scaly friends are buried. Among the dearly departed are Topper (Hopalong Cassidy's horse), Lassie, the MGM lion, Rudolf Valentino's dog, Stephen Spielberg's dog, and Mae West's monkey.

WHEN David Bates lost his dearest friend, His Most Gracious Majesty the Lord Grimsley of Katmandu, as the result of a drug overdose in 1974, he decided that the least he could do to repay the years of joy and companionship was to provide a funeral fit for a king. Lord Grimsley lay in state for three weeks on a bed of silk, before being buried in a casket decorated with 1,000 carnations. The funeral orations included readings from the poetry of Wordsworth and Shelley. Costing over £2,500, it was probably the most lavish and expensive funeral ever held for a parrot.

They Went Thataway

VICTORIA Woodhull, a nineteenth-century radical feminist, was convinced that she would die if she went to bed in her old age. She spent the last four years of her life sitting in a chair, finally dying at the age of eighty-nine, in 1927.

THE Athenian tragic poet Aeschylus died as tragically as he lived, if legend is to be believed. The story goes that he was killed when a butter-fingered eagle dropped the tortoise he was carrying onto Aeschylus's head, killing him instantly.

IN the American Wild West being dragged by a horse while caught in the stirrups was a more common cause of death than being shot in a gun battle.

WILD Bill Hickok, Al Jolson and Buster Keaton all died while playing cards.

MARSHALL Gambrell was killed on his way to visit relatives in Connecticut when he lost control of his car, crashed into a cemetery, and was hurled from the car into a marble headstone.

SPONTANEOUS combustion is the name of the strange phenomenon when a human body suddenly ignites and burns without any known external cause. The combustion of Mrs Mary Carpenter took place right in front of her husband while they were holidaying on a cabin cruiser. She was sipping a drink in the lounge when she suddenly burst into flames. In the last 400 years, over 200 similarly volatile cases have been reported.

WHEN New York Metropolitan opera star tenor Richard Versalle sang the words 'You can only live so long' in the opera *The Makropulos Affair*, they proved to be strangely prophetic. As he finished singing the words, he collapsed and died.

INSEPARABLE identical twins William and John Bloomfield, aged sixty-one, died within minutes of each other while watching television together.

WHEN John Cratcher's doctors told him they had found a suitable heart for his long-awaited heart transplant operation, the shock killed him. The surgeons later admitted to his distressed widow that the heart would not have been suitable for him, after all.

AMERICAN nutrition expert J. I. Rodale tempted fate just a little too far when he was being interviewed on a US talk show. Immediately after boasting 'I'm so healthy I expect to live on and on' he dropped dead of a heart attack.

WILLIAM the Conqueror was proud of the fact that he could jump on to a saddled horse wearing full armour. He died of injuries received from a saddle pommel. Ouch!

SEVERAL mystery deaths were reported at the Pelanomi Hospital in Bloemfontein, in South Africa's Orange Free State. It seems that every Friday, over the period of several months during 1994, hospital staff found the patient occupying a certain bed in the intensive care unit lying dead, with no apparent cause. Doctors feared an unknown killer disease.

The mystery was solved when a nurse saw the Friday morning cleaner enter the ward, unplug the life-support system beside the bed, plug in her floor polisher, and proceed to clean the ward. She had been doing this for some months, plugging in the life-support machine when she had finished, and leaving no clues as to the cause of the deaths.

Grave Difficulties

NEWLY widowed Stella Serth of Tasmania was fined £200 for dancing on her husband's grave and singing 'Who's Sorry Now?'.

OPERATORS of the Rosemount Memorial Park Cemetery in New Jersey have confessed to burying some people under pavements, and promised that in the future they would not inter people more than five deep in a single grave. They were fined by the State Division of Consumer Affairs, and were told: 'You are not supposed to bury people under sidewalks. The bereaved did not expect that their loved ones would find eternal rest under a pathway.'

WHEN Larry Bojarski failed to pay a funeral home in Richmond, Texas, within the promised three days, instead of sending a reminder note, the Evans Mortuary dumped his father's body on his porch – nude and covered with a sheet.

Celestial Bodies

BEN Jonson, the poet and playwright, was buried in a standing position. He had chosen his burial place in Westminster Cathedral at the request of King Charles I, who personally promised him that the spot would remain his. However, after Jonson's death in 1637, it was found that the space he had selected already had a previous occupant, except for about eighteen inches of spare ground. The coffin was therefore placed in an upright position.

But there is a less romantic explanation for the poet's vertical burial – Jonson died in poverty and it is possible that he was buried upright not only to save space, but expense too.

ARCHDUKE Ferdinand of Austria was undone by his own vanity. When he was going to attend a great state occasion, he would have himself sewn into his uniform so there would not be one crease to be seen. When he was shot in Sarajevo in 1914, doctors could not unbutton his uniform, and by the time scissors were found, Ferdinand had bled to death.

FILM star Bela Lugosi was buried in the cape that he wore in his Count Dracula role. Appropriately, he died while reading a script entitled 'The Final Curtain'.

HUMPHREY Bogart was buried with a whistle. A special memento from his wife Lauren Bacall's role in *To Have and Have Not* – not only her first film, but also the first of many films in which the couple starred together – it was inscribed with her legendary line – 'If you need anything, just whistle'.

THE bones of Queen Boadicea, queen of the English Iceni tribe, who died in 60 AD, are said to lie somewhere beneath platform ten of King's Cross Station.

THE Holy Roman Emperor Charlemagne was buried in 814 AD sitting on a marble throne with a crown on his head, a globe in one hand, a sceptre in the other, and an imperial robe over his shoulders.

ANYONE digging beneath the Bank of England may be surprised to find – instead of giant mounds of gold – a giant. Jenkins, who was eight foot tall requested that he be buried there in order that his body be kept from body snatchers. When he died in 1798, his request was granted.

LORD Nelson chose to be buried in St Paul's Church in London rather than in Westminster Abbey because he believed that Westminster was sinking into the nearby River Thames.

ORVILLE and Wilbur Wright are famous as the first people to fly an aeroplane. What is less well known is that Orville was also the pilot of the plane in which the first flying fatality occurred. Five years after his historic flight, he was accompanied by Lieutenant Thomas E. Selfridge of the US Signal Corps when, in mid-flight, the propeller broke and the plane plunged 150 feet. Selfridge was killed, and Orville suffered multiple hip and leg fractures.

Bring Out Your Dead

IN Madagascar, people regularly treat their dead relatives to a day out. They believe in honouring the dead by treating them as though they are still alive. If a corpse is interred in a simple grave, the remains will be exhumed perhaps years after death, wrapped in a fresh silk shroud, and placed in the tomb of the kin group. Even if the body has been resting in the proper place from the time of the original funeral, it will still be re-shrouded at a later date. On that occasion, even older corpses that have already been buried will be removed, danced with, sung to, and toured around the locality before they too are re-shrouded and replaced.

THE Malagasy Indians of Madagascar like to toss their dead. Every few years, they dig up their dead, put them in the sunlight for a while, then toss them up and catch them. They then wrap them in new silk garments and re-bury them.

Upper Crust

WHEN Judge Theodore Sedgwick, a statesman and jurist, died, he was buried under a high granite obelisk in the centre of the graveyard in Stockbridge, Massachusetts. His wife, Pamela, was buried beside him, and their seven children are buried in a circle around them. Their children, in turn, are buried around them in another circle and so on, circle by circle throughout the generations. They are all buried facing towards the judge. It is known as the Sedgwick Pie, and Judge Theodore planned this so that on Judgement Day, when all the Sedgwicks rise up, each will face another Sedgwick, and will not have to see the ordinary folks lying outside the circle.

For a Few Dollars More . . .

A funeral home in Florida organizes cruises to the Bahamas to help mourners get over their grief.

AT the Cedar Park Cemetery and Funeral Home in Chicago, the feeling is that death can be fun. The cemetery sponsors a ten-kilometre 'Heaven Can Wait' run on the cemetery grounds, an ice-sculpture contest and an Easter egg hunt. They even give discounts on burials and funerals based on the number of points scored by the city's professional basketball team, the Chicago Bulls.

NATIONAL Music Service Corporation in America have introduced The Tribute Programme, a six-minute replay of the deceased's life to be shown at the funeral. It features snapshots of the guest of honour that dissolve to scenes of mountains, seashores, forests, or any of hundreds of stock video images in the library. The family selects the backgrounds and chooses a piece of music from the song rack, and a quotation that appears at the end of the programme.

IN Pompano Beach, Florida, people can make sure they have the last word. The Eternal Monument Company offers a service whereby a customer can have himself filmed and his voice taped to be played at the funeral. Copies of the tape are given to the guests as a lasting memento.

R.I.P. – Finally

CHRISTOPHER Columbus, the great explorer who discovered America, continued to travel widely even after his death on 20 May 1506. He was first buried at the Church of San Francisco in Valladolid in Spain, but his body was moved in 1513, by order of his patron Don Diego, to a chapel in the monastery of Santa Maria de las Cuevas, Seville. Then, in 1542, his bones, along with his son's, were taken to Santo Domingo and interred before the high altar of the cathedral. When Santa Domingo was ceded to the French in 1795, Columbus's remains were moved to Havana. When Cuba became independent, Columbus was returned to Spain and put in a monument in Seville Cathedral.

It seems no one ever considered burying him in Genoa, Italy, the city of his birth, and where to this day he is celebrated as her most famous son.

E MPEROR Haile Selassie of Ethiopia took some time to rest in peace. He died in 1975 at the age of eighty-three, it is believed at the hands of an assassin, and was buried under the office floor of former president Haile Mariam Mengistu, the man who overthrew him. He was apparently put there to ensure that the body did not rise from the dead. He was eventually re-buried at the Orthodox Cathedral.

W HEN a Romanian man died in Bucharest, his three nephews could not afford to pay for a hearse to take their uncle's body the 300 miles to the family graveyard in Caransebes. So they bought four train tickets, doused their uncle with alcohol to conceal the smell, and told the conductor he was dead drunk.

T HE body of John Paul Jones, a hero of the American revolution, had a less than heroic time as a result of bureaucratic error. His body was mislaid for 113 years. When he died in Paris, he was embalmed in preparation for his return to America and a hero's funeral. Then he was somehow forgotten, and the French quietly buried him.

Sometime later, in the early years of the twentieth century, the US Government suddenly remembered poor John, and decided to return him at last to his homeland. However, the French cemetery where he was buried had long since become a commercial development. The Americans managed to find an old map, and employed a squad of miners who, by tunnelling through hundreds of feet of drains, cellars and foundations, eventually found our hero's coffin, marked with the initials JPJ. On opening the casket, he was found to be remarkably well preserved, though his nose had been squashed by the coffin lid. He was finally laid to rest in the US Naval College at Annapolis, Maryland.

ALEXANDER T. Stewart, a successful New York merchant, died in 1876, and was buried in St Mark's Church in New York City. Two years later the coffin was removed and the body held for a ransom of $200,000. After three years of negotiation (the one good thing about a corpse kidnapping is there is no time pressure!) the family paid a small portion of the ransom demand and the body was returned.

IT was nineteen years after his death in 1821 before Napoleon was finally laid to rest. He was first buried on the island of St Helena, where he spent the last six years of his life. His grave was marked by a stone bearing no name, only the words 'Here rests'. His body was finally returned to his beloved France in 1840, where he was re-interred in the Hotel des Invalides, although Napoleon had left instructions that his body be cremated. Another request of his was honoured, however. His head was shaved and his hair was divided amongst his friends.

There's a Body in the Trunk!

THE body of the great seventeenth-century religious emancipator Roger Williams was eaten by a tree. Williams died in 1683 and was buried in a poorly marked grave in the backyard of his home in Providence, Rhode Island. Fifty-six years later, grave-diggers accidentally broke into the emancipator's coffin while excavating a nearby grave, exposing the bones. In 1860, a descendant of Williams, Stephen Randall, ordered a workman to exhume the remains from the plot and transfer them to a more suitable tomb. But the excavation yielded only a few rusted coffin nails and scraps of rotten wood. Not a bone was found.

What the workman did find was something extraordinary.

The root of a nearby apple tree lay exactly where the remains should have been, and it had taken the shape of Williams's body, from head to heels. As it grew, the root had encountered Williams's skull and followed the path of least resistance, inching down the side of his head, backbone, hips and legs, moulding itself closely to the contours of his body. The corpse itself was gone – absorbed into the tree through the roots. The human-shaped root was removed for safekeeping and today is on display at the Rhode Island Historical Society.

HANS Wilhelm von Thummel, a romantic poet, actually chose a fate similar to that of Roger Williams. He was laid to rest in the hollow of an oak tree on 1 March 1824, in Noebdenitz, Germany. The tree is still living, and has long since enclosed the poet's body.

A Fine and Private Place

THE word sarcophagus comes from the Greek for 'flesh eater'. It was believed that the container devoured the flesh of the corpse inside it.

PRIOR to today's advanced medical techniques of determining brain death, a society was formed for the Prevention of People Being Buried Alive. Fearful that those falling into a coma or other states simulating death could regain consciousness after burial, they devised an alarm system utilizing a bell and a piece of string. The ill-fated and, one would suspect, quite bewildered victim of circumstance could then simply yank the string, thereby ringing a bell at the surface. The society's last known member was buried over a hundred years ago. Since no one has heard from him since, we can assume he was a dead ringer.

LARYEA Okai is a master coffin-maker in Ghana, and specializes in carved and painted designer coffins. Customers can choose from a selection of designs, including a taxi, gigantic coffin-sized crabs and lobsters, pods of cocoa and ears of corn. Families will often choose designs reflecting the profession or personality of the deceased. A loaf of bread might be the choice for a baker, a fish for a fisherman, a huge hen for the mother of a large family. Moses Obroa, the head of a small Ghanaian fishing fleet, was buried in a giant sardine-shaped coffin. Businessmen have been sent off in Mercedes cars with RIP number-plates, and a pilot chose to reach for the skies in a plane with spinning propellers.

Mr Okai's competitor down the road is Paa Joe, who has been building designer coffins for nineteen years. He was once asked to make a coffin for a very popular lorry driver. The man's colleagues insisted that he build a lorry complete with all the wiring, a horn, headlights, a radio and cassette player, even a light on the top. He did so, but informed them that once the battery had run down, there was nothing he could do about it. Some of his customers, who were never able to travel in this life, decided to depart for the next life in scale models of planes. One of the most popular models is an Air Canada jet, seemingly ready for take-off.

At some funerals of wealthier folks, special cloth is printed bearing the likeness of the deceased, to be worn by all who take part in the funeral.

AMERICANS love their cars so much, coffin manufacturers even reflect the latest automotive shapes and colours in their own line of work. The Aurora Casket Company have yearly reviews on what car preferences will be. Pinstriping, for instance, has recently been introduced. Balanced Line Caskets manufacture coffins which follow Cadillac's colours. They have just introduced a 'fire mist' finish, with a metal flake that illuminates when light hits it. Some coffins feature an interior of kid leather simulating interiors of a Mercedes or BMW. They are currently planning a Laura Ashley interior too. Personalized interiors are also popular, particularly in rental caskets, which are becoming common as cremation rates rise – a new interior is snapped in with Velcro after each use. Examples of interiors include embroidered US flags, wedding rings, and even a large coloured trout for the fishing fanatic.

I N 1932, S. P. Dinsmoor of Lucas, Kansas, died at the age of eighty-nine. He had given many years to the making of a concrete Garden of Eden in which he had built his own tomb and prescribed the manner of his own burial. Using 2273 bags of cement, Dinsmoor constructed a two-storey cement house, a cement tree of life guarded by a cement angel, a cement devil high in another cement tree, cement images of Adam and Eve, and, of course, a cement serpent. In the mausoleum, which rises to a height of forty feet, are cement coffins for himself and his wife. On the top of his coffin is a plate-glass lid which serves two purposes. As Dinsmoor wrote:

'I have a will that none except my wife, my descendants, their husbands and wives, shall go in to see me for less than a \$1. That will pay some one to look after the place, and I promise everyone that comes in to see me (they can look through the plate glass and . . . see my face) that if I see them dropping a dollar in the hands of the flunky, and I see the dollar, I will give them a smile . . . It seems to me that people buried in iron and wooden boxes will be frying and burning up in the resurrection morn. How will they get out when this world is on fire? Cement will not stand fire, the glass will break. This cement lid will fly open and I will sail out like a locust.'

MILLIONAIRE Sandra West of San Antonio, Texas, who died in 1977, decided it was simply not fitting to be buried in a common old coffin. So, she went to meet her Maker in her nightdress, sitting in the front seat of her much loved blue Ferrari.

ALONZO Lyman Credle, who died in 1884 at the age of thirty-four, arranged to be buried upright. He had suffered from asthma for many years and had only been able to rest in an upright position. He reckoned that for him, rest in peace could only be fulfilled – as in life – upright.

ALICE Whitfield of Aberdeen, Mississippi, was buried, as she requested, in a mausoleum, sitting upright in her favourite rocking chair. Reuben Smith was buried in a tomb in Amesbury, Massachusetts, seated in a chair, before a table on which rested his pipe, a newspaper and a chess board. He reportedly offered a substantial sum to any woman who would spend one night with his corpse in the tomb, but it seems there were no takers.

JIMMY Dale Stubble, a cowboy from Grand Junction, Colorado, was paralysed from the neck down as a result of a fight with another cowboy. He decided that, though he might have to spend the rest of his life sitting in a wheelchair or lying flat on his back, there was no reason for him to spend eternity the same way; so when he died his will specified he was to be buried standing up. Jimmy's friends dressed him in full cowboy regalia, including his Stetson hat and his boots. His saddle-draped coffin was taken in a pick-up truck to the graveyard where it was lowered, feet first, into the ground.

BLACKBIRD, a Chief of the Omaha Indian tribe, spent most of his waking hours on his horses. His last was his favourite, so Blackbird gave instructions that when he died, he was to be buried sitting on his beloved horse. Unfortunately for the horse, Blackbird died first.

The Ultimate High

TIMOTHY Leary, the drugs guru of the sixties, planned to be even more spaced-out in death than he was in life. He had originally intended to be frozen in a cryonics laboratory, but changed his mind at the thought that he might be awoken in fifty years, not by a kiss, but 'surrounded by people with clipboards and no sense of humour'. A fate worse than death for the fun-loving Professor Leary! So, when he died in 1996, he made arrangements for his ashes to be launched into space. A Texas company, Celestis Inc, which organizes 'post cremation memorialization opportunities in space', will send his ashes, along with those of eleven other travellers, into space. Friends and relatives will be invited to attend the launch, and will be offered a complimentary video. Long after his death, Timothy Leary will still be on the ultimate trip.

One of the other travellers on this eternal journey will be Gene Roddenberry, the creator of *Star Trek*.

The Last Laugh

M AD Jack Fuller loved a good wager and practical jokes. The 300-pound politician, who was MP for Sussex from 1801 to 1812, built a number of monuments which give testimony to his very special *joie de vivre* but his greatest folly was his last.

In an arrangement with the minister of his church, he agreed to relocate a pub one mile down the road from its position facing the church. In exchange he was to be allowed to build the tomb of his choice for his future burial in the churchyard. To the minister it seemed a reasonable proposal. For Fuller it was a dream too good to be true. Fuller hired Sir Robert Smirke, architect of the British Museum, to design and construct his mausoleum. Always larger than life, both in girth and in attitude, Fuller had Smirke design a two-storey pyramid. He wanted a chamber inside big enough for him to be buried sitting upright wearing a top hat, with a roast chicken and a bottle of good red wine on a table in front of him. Broken glass was to be scattered throughout to stop the devil from disturbing Jack's eternal feast. The pyramid was constructed, taking up a good portion of the graveyard and competing for attention with the tiny country church.

For years after Mad Jack's death his monumental mound continued to be a subject of controversy. There was even some talk of replacing it with a more discreet memorial, but before proceeding along those lines, it was decided to open the tomb and see how Mad Jack was doing. What did they find? Nothing. No table, no chicken, no wine, no top hat – and no Jack Fuller. Some people said he was buried in a grave underneath the tomb, but for others it was Mad Jack's final joke – he built the most talked about tomb in the county and wasn't even in it.

The pyramid can still be seen in the Brightling churchyard today. As for Jack, he's probably still having a good laugh . . . somewhere.

WEALTHY Canadian lawyer Charles Millar died in 1928 at the age of seventy-three, and left a will full of practical jokes. To a judge and a preacher, both of whom were fanatically opposed to gambling, he left shares in a race-track which included automatic membership in the Jockey Club. To a group of ministers opposed to drinking, he left $50,000 in shares in a brewery – all but one of the teetotallers accepted the bequest. Three of his friends, all of whom loathed each other, were bequeathed his holiday home in Jamaica, which they had to share.

But the most controversial of his bequests was that the Toronto woman who 'has given birth to the greatest number of children at the expiration of ten years from my death' would receive a part of his fortune. Within nine months, Toronto maternity hospitals were reporting a significant increase in business. Finally, on 30 May 1938, Judge MacDonnell of Toronto's Surrogate Court awarded the cash estate of $568,106. Two women received a consolation prize of $12,500, but the bulk was split equally between four mothers, each of whom gave birth to nine children during the specified ten years. On receipt of the bequest, each of the four women vowed to practise birth control.

TO the tenth Duke of Hamilton, dying was no laughing matter. In fact, he felt it would be demeaning for his aristocratic bones to be buried in a conventional coffin. So he outbid the British Museum and bought a sarcophagus thought to belong to an Egyptian princess. The Duke's dreams of being buried like royalty were to become a nightmare.

As he lay dying, it was brought to his attention that his glorified resting chamber was a foot too short. To this the Duke replied, 'Well then, double me up!'. After he died, it soon became apparent that his stiff, and rather rotund, body was not going to double as he had envisioned. In order to be placed in his prized sarcophagus, his feet had to be cut off. A short time afterwards, the British Museum notified the Duke's estate that the sarcophagus was not formerly that of an Egyptian princess, but of a court jester.

When Death Us Do Part

A loving widow in Mawuggwe village in Uganda dreamt that her husband complained to her that his grave was cold, and asked her to be dug up to lie in the sun. She now exhumes his body every day, takes it home to enjoy the sunshine, then returns it to the grave until the next day.

Q UEEN Victoria's grief at the death of her beloved Albert is legendary. Every day, from the day he died, she ordered that his evening clothes be laid, freshly pressed, on his bed at Windsor Castle.

I NES de Castro was the beautiful mistress to Portugal's future King Pedro I. She was murdered in 1355, and entombed by Pedro in the abbey church at Alcobaca. When Pedro's father died, and he became king, he decided that the only woman suitable to be his queen was poor Ines, who had been dead for more than two years. He had her exhumed, propped on a lavish throne, and dressed in magnificent coronation robes.

Portugal's clergy, nobility and commoners had to pay homage to the corpse, kissing her bony hands. She sat through the coronation banquet, and was finally returned to her tomb after dark in a chariot drawn by six black mules in a procession lighted by 500 candles.

D R Katuabruo Miyamoto of Japan loved his wife so much, he just could not bear to be parted from her. When she died in 1959, he embalmed her body and slept next to her every night for ten years. When police discovered his bizarre bedmate, she was buried, and he was fined £2,000 for failing to report a death.

Grave Concerns

H ENRY Trigg, of Hitchin in Hertfordshire became deter-mined after disturbing grave-robbers as he walked through a graveyard one night that his body would rest in peace. Before he died in 1722, Trigg came up with a lofty idea and jotted it into his will. He gave his brother his worldly earnings on the condition that he build a loft in the rafters of the old barn behind his house and put his coffin within it. The instructions were followed to the letter. When the coffin was opened by distant relatives in 1831, Trigg was none the worse for wear.

Trigg remained undisturbed until World War I, when Australian soldiers billeted in the barn discovered the coffin. In it they found Henry Trigg. What could be more suitable to take back to Australia as a memento of their stay in England?

The empty coffin can still be seen lying on the rafters of the barn in Hitchin. As for Henry Trigg, he avoided being dissected in an English medical school only to end up as a souvenir in Australia.

Gone but Not Forgotten

THERE are few more bizarre and startling memorials than that of Lady Sarah Hare. Legend has it that while sewing on a Sunday, a sacrilegious practice in the 1700s, Sarah accidentally pricked herself on the finger with a needle. She died soon afterward of blood poisoning. Her loving brother had a life-sized wax figure of Sarah placed in a mahogany case in the family chapel in the Church of the Holy Trinity in Stow Bardolph, Norfolk. The wax figure of Sarah Hare can still be seen there, dressed in the very clothes in which she died.

RAY Tse loved cars and, ironically, was killed in a car crash in 1980. His loving brother, David, decided he should have the kind of gravestone he would have liked, so Ray's New York grave is decorated with a seventeen-foot granite replica of a Mercedes Benz 240-D built from real Mercedes blueprints. The dead man's name is carved into the number plate.

ARCHIE Arnold's grave in Fort Wayne, Texas, is flanked by two parking meters, each displaying the sign 'Expired'.

IN Pennsylvania, there is a gravestone which reads: 'Here lies the body of Jonathan Blake. Stepped on the gas instead of the brake.'

ON the tomb of a nagging wife in the US:
'Beneath this stone, a lump of clay, Lies Arabella Young,
Who, on the twenty-fourth of May, Began to hold her tongue.'

A somewhat bitter reproach to the US government appears
on this gravestone in Pennsylvania:

RANSOM BEARDSLEY
Died Jan 24 1850
Aged 56 years 7 months 21 days
A volunteer in the war of 1812
No pension

Reading tombstones shows that the old Wild West really was
pretty wild. Here are some examples:

GEORGE JOHNSON
Hanged by mistake

SIX SHOOTER JIM – 1885
Shot by Burt Alvord

In Boothill Cemetery of Tombstone, Arizona, the following
epitaphs can be found:

Murdered on the streets of Tombstone
(several)

or:

BRONCO CHARLIE
Shot by Ormsby

And nearby:

RED RIVER TOM
Shot by Ormsby

SMALLPOX deaths were once so common that victims were sometimes treated with less respect than we would now consider suitable:

Cut into a rock near Boston Harbour –

Nearby these gray rocks
Enclos'd in a box
Lies Hatter Cox
Who died of smallpox

And it seems that inoculation sometimes killed rather than cured. Jonathan Tute died in 1763, and was buried in North Cemetery, Vernon, Vermont. His tombstone reads:

But tho' His Spirits fled on high
His body mould'ring here must lie
Behold the amazing alteration
Effected by Inoculation
The means Employed his Life to save
Hurried Him Headlong to the Grave

BODY snatching was a common problem. Poor Ruth Sprague died in 1816 and was buried in Hoosick Falls, New York. Roderick R. Clow, a student, exhumed the grave, and removed the body to a local doctor's laboratory. The remains were recovered, and Ruth's angry family decided to erect this stone:

She was stolen from the grave
by Roderick R. Clow & dissected
at Dr P. M. Armstrong's office
in Hoosick, NY from which place
her mutilated remains were
obtained and deposited here.
Her body dissected by fiendish Men
Her bones anatomized,
her soul we trust has risen to God
Where few Physicians rise.

POOR Lochart Tindall, who died in 1799, was killed when
he fell head first into the hopper of a cider mill:

The apple wheel did roll on me
And by it I was slain,
But Christ has bought my liberty,
In Him I'll rise again.

IN Mount Pleasant Cemetery, New Jersey:

ANDREW C. HAND
Born March 12th 1842
that Cherry Tree of luscious fruit
beguiled him too high a branch did break
and down he fell and broke his neck and
died July 13th, 1862

IN Elmwood Cemetery, Holyoke, Massachusetts:

IN MEMORY OF MR NATH. PARKS,

Aged 19, who on
21st March 1794
Being out a hunting
and conceal'd
in a Ditch was
Casually shot by
Mr Luther
Frink

AN epitaph in Girard, Pennsylvania, states:

IN MEMORY OF
ELLEN SHANNON

Aged 26 years
Who was fatally burned
March 21st 1870
by the explosion of a lamp
filled with 'R. E. Danforth's
Non Explosive
Burning Fluid'

THE family of Warren Gibbs had their revenge on his murdering wife. On his tombstone in Knight's Corner Burying Ground, Pelham, Massachusetts:

WARREN GIBBS

died by arsenic poison
Mar 23 1860.
Age 36 yrs. 5 mos.
23 dys.
Think my friends when this you see

How my wife hath dealt by me
She in some oysters did prepare
Some poison for my lot and share
Then of the same I did partake
And nature yielded to its fate
Before she my wife became
Mary Felton was her name.
Erected by his Brother
Wm. Gibbs.

THE notorious outlaw Jesse James was buried twice – first on 3 April 1882, after being shot by a member of his gang, who was tempted by the $10,000 reward. His mother erected a stone which read:

IN LOVING MEMORY OF MY BELOVED SON
JESSE W. JAMES
Died April 3, 1882
Aged 34 Years, 6 Months, 28 Days
Murdered by a Traitor and Coward Whose
Name Is Not Worthy to Appear Here.

Twenty years later, he was exhumed, and this famous outlaw was buried with full military honours. It seems that Jesse James had been engaged in guerrilla activities during the Civil War.

But poor Jesse just doesn't seem able to rest in peace. His body has recently been exhumed again, this time to find out if the body in question really is Jesse James.

BENJAMIN Franklin, despite his great work as President of Pennsylvania, and as ambassador to the Court of France, never forgot his true profession – that of printer. He would therefore have been pleased to see that his inscription bore symbols of his trade:

> BENJAMIN FRANKLIN, *a * in his profession;*
> *the type of honesty; and ! of all; and*
> *although the (pointing finger) of death put a . to his*
> *existence, each (Section mark) of his life is without*
> *an =*

THOMAS Campbell of Chicago was a travelling salesman. He took his profession seriously so when he died in 1862, and was buried in Aspen Grove Cemetery, Burlington, Iowa, his stone was inscribed:

> *My Trip is Ended.*
> *Send My Samples Home.*

COMMERCE entered into the final monument of Jane Smith also, whose husband just happened to be a stone cutter. Her stone, in Springdale, Ohio, reads:
    'Here lies Jane Smith, wife of Thomas Smith, marble cutter. This monument was erected by her husband as a tribute to her memory and a specimen of his work. Monuments of the same style 350 dollars.'

The Last Supper

THOMAS Parr was born in the parish of Alberbury Shropshire, in 1483 during the reign of King Edward V. A simple farmer, he lived through the reigns of Richard III, Henry

VII, Henry VIII, Edward IV and Queen Mary. He was seventy-five when Elizabeth I came to the throne in 1558 and five years later he married for the first time.

When Queen Elizabeth died and was succeeded on the throne by James I, it made no difference to Thomas Parr. He outlived his first wife and got married again at the ripe old age of 122. He outlived this wife too as well as his children and grandchildren by his first wife.

In 1635, when Parr was 152, King Charles I heard of Parr's astounding longevity and invited him to London for a royal feast. Before dinner, the king asked Parr the secret of long life. Simple meals of grains and meats, said Parr. The king offered Parr goose livers and baby eels basted in butter and onions, followed by fried sheeps' eyeballs. The banquet continued for hours, Parr regaling the king with stories, the king seeing to it that Parr's plate and glass were always full. Unfortunately Parr, probably overwhelmed by the activity and certainly the food, expired at the table. The distraught king, feeling responsible for Old Parr's demise, had him buried in Westminster Abbey, among the royal and noble dead of England. The inscription on his plaque in Thomas Parr's church states, 'He lived 152 years, through the reigns of ten Monarchs.' What it doesn't say is he died from eating food fit for a king!

The City of the Dead

WHEN the major infrastructure that is now metropolitan Paris was being built, the stone used came from limestone quarries beneath the city. Eventually, the buildings began to collapse into the cavernous catacombs below, so the digging ended, but Paris continued to grow until eventually there seemed to be no more space available for expansion. By 1786, the space problem had become such that the city's leaders decided to empty the ancient cemeteries and build on them. So the bones were dug up and relocated in the vast unused quarries beneath the streets of the Latin Quarter.

The bones were moved in funeral carts, accompanied by priests, in the dead of night, and unceremoniously dumped in huge piles over an area of dozens of square miles one hundred and fifty feet below Paris's teeming streets and alleyways.

It wasn't until the reign of Louis Napoleon that some thought was given to the desecration. Workmen and artisans decorated miles and miles of the walls of the catacombs with bones and skulls. Today Paris has a population of 9 million above ground and another 6 million below its streets, whose bones make up the most bizarre mosaic in the world.

Remains of the Day

JEREMY Bentham, the father of Utilitarianism and one of the founders of the University of London, may be considered the eccentric's eccentric.

In his treatise 'Auto Icon, or the Uses of the Dead to the Living', he suggested that dead bodies should be embalmed and varnished so that everyone could be their own statue, or auto-icon. The embalmed corpses, he suggested, could be used to decorate people's gardens and remind their descendants of their forebears. He wrote, 'If a country gentleman has rows of trees leading to his dwelling, the auto-icons of his family might alternate with the trees.'

Consistent with his theory, Bentham conceived a way to amaze people even after he was dead. He left his entire estate to University College on the following basis: that he be publicly dissected in front of his friends, then stuffed, dressed in his finest clothes, and mounted in a chair. He ordered that his walking stick, which he affectionately called 'Dapple' be placed in his hand.

Furthermore Bentham's will stated he must continue to attend the annual meeting of the University's Board of Governors. Since his death in 1832, Jeremy Bentham has never missed a meeting. He is listed in the minutes as 'present, but not voting'.

THE Russians' claim that they have a secret method of embalming which has ensured the preservation of Lenin's body could be considered dubious to say the least. Dr Sergei S. Debov, when he revealed the well-kept secret, explained that a secret embalming compound was used to replace all the water in the Russian leader's skin. His body is kept at sixteen degrees Celsius, and seventy per cent humidity. Numerous sensors and monitors around the body are constantly checked by a permanent staff of ten specialists. Lenin's hands and face are regularly bathed in embalming fluid, and his body is completely immersed in the fluid every five years.

However, some visitors to the great mausoleum in Moscow, who were perhaps a little more cynical (and a little more observant) than the average awestruck Russian, have noticed that Lenin may be crumbling along with his political legacy. One viewer was filing past the dimly lit casket and was horrified to see Lenin's ear drop off. There was much consternation, and the mausoleum was immediately closed. It is now widely believed that the magical 'secret embalming fluid' did not work too well, and Lenin's body is now approximately sixty per cent wax – including the rogue ear, which was stuck on in time for the next parade of visitors.

Lenin's final ignominy, however, is that his body is kept at the required temperature not by a sophisticated cooling machinery, but by way of a West German fish freezing plant. How the mighty are fallen!

I N Bangladore, a servant proved to be so indispensable that when he died, he was stuffed and displayed in the palace of his master, the Maharajah of Mysore. There is an inscription on the glass case containing his remains which states, 'He had started as an under gardener, risen to head gardener, and then been made footman. He had given twenty-seven years loyal service.' It seems the Maharajah just couldn't let good help go.

One Last Thing

W HEN Irish grandmother Johanna Connors died aged seventy, she wanted her grieving friends and relatives to have a good time. So, her last wish was to have her coffin carried to her favourite pubs in England, and then returned to Ireland for burial. The wake started at 8.30 am at the Marlbrook pub in Bromsgrove and ended twelve hours later at the Bull Inn at Haverfordwest.

A FTER a lifetime of service to King Charles I, Sir Nicholas Crispe made a last request that his heart be buried at the feet of his master. So, while Sir Nicholas's cadaver lies outside the church, his heart reposes in an urn below a bust of the King. Crispe also asked that on the anniversary of the heart's entombment it should be removed from the urn and refreshed with a glass of wine.

THE family of the eighteenth Earl of Derby fulfilled his last request by bearing his coffin to church on a trailer drawn by a red tractor. The late peer disliked hearses.

THE last wish of the Indian ruler Khan Jahan was to be buried in a conical tomb, and to have his hand extending out of it – so that he could continue his favourite pastime of shaking hands even after his death.

VICTOR Browning's dying wish was to ride in his baby-blue Cadillac from Wimberley to his nephew's crematorium in California. So, the day after he died at the age of eighty-three, Browning's son and grandson strapped his embalmed body in the back seat of the 1990 Seville and drove 1,300 miles to California. According to his son, they were stopped by a border guard, who asked his father how he was doing. The son said, 'Oh, he's been sleeping since we left Texas.' The officer said, 'Well, he sure is sleeping sound,' and waved them across the border.

WHEN Mrs Martin Van Butchell died in 1775, her will mandated that her husband was not to receive his large inheritance unless her body remained above ground. In order to fulfil his wife's last wishes, he had her embalmed. He then dressed her in her finest clothing and put her on display in the family parlour. He held daily visiting hours for her former friends. Needless to say, he received her estate.

Her friends were so impressed with her condition that word of her preserved state spread. Soon others were having their dearly departed embalmed and the process became fashionable in Europe for the first time. Undertakers skilled in the art even went on tour with their prize corpses, displaying them in shop windows, county fairs and music hall lobbies, creating a thriving business for themselves. Ironically, Mrs Van Butchell's end began a new industry.

Ashes to . . .

A Californian psychiatrist and frisbee fanatic has requested that on his death he be cremated and his ashes mixed with polyethylene, which should then be formed into twenty-five professional model frisbees.

D H. Lawrence seems to have been as unlucky in love – and death – as some of the characters in his novels. After his death, his mistress Frieda inadvertently left his ashes on a Mexican railway platform while en route to meet her Italian lover, Angelo Ravagli. The urn, once retrieved, was then stolen by a rival lover. The careless Frieda managed to get the ashes back once again, and decided to ensure they would never again be lost – so she had them shovelled into a concrete mixer and included them in a slab which was being made for her new mantelpiece.

W HEN Frank Goldsworthy died in Florida in 1982, he left instructions that his ashes be scattered in the Atlantic – he had managed to escape the Titanic when she sank in 1912, but his father had been one of the many victims. He wanted, finally, to be reunited.

IF Steve Vaughn of Phoenix, Arizona, becomes successful, instead of wearing our hearts on our sleeves, we could be wearing our loved ones round our necks! He has formed a company called Sunset Pathways – America Inc, and is working on a method whereby their ashes will be compressed and converted into carbon graphite. He could then synthesize a diamond which could be worn as a constant reminder of the dear departed.

CREMATION urns made by Californian sculptor Al Honig feature strobe lights, moving parts, music and sometimes even titles such as 'Those Who Live by the Sword' which features an antique brandy bottle housed in an old liquor bottle cabinet; it plays 'How Dry I Am' when the lid is opened.

TRUMAN Capote willed that his ashes be divided in half after his death. One half went to his companion, Jack Dunphy, while the other half went to his friend, the talk show host Johnny Carson. Unfortunately, during a 1988 Halloween party, one of the Carsons' guests absconded with the ashes, and they have never been found. So, at least half of Truman Capote rests in peace.

FANS of the Ajax football club can look forward to being more than lifetime members of the supporters' club. Some of the hallowed turf has been transferred to a nearby crematorium so that fans can have their ashes scattered over their heroes' ground without making a mess of the pitch!

Last Will and Testament

IN his will, William Shakespeare left his wife, Anne Hathaway, his 'second best bed'.

IT is generally believed that wills have to be written on parchment or paper. In fact many wills have been written on such things as a girl's portrait, a shirt front, eggshells, gramophone records, furniture and pebbles. More than one man has actually had his will tattooed.

ONE business executive, who had always wanted to be on the stage, left his fortune to a theatre for acting scholarships, with the proviso that his corpse be decapitated, the flesh removed from his skull, and his bleached cranium used as the skull of the jester Yorick in *Hamlet*. His wishes were complied with.

A WEALTHY banker had the last word when he cut two people out of his will. 'To my wife and her lover, I leave the knowledge that I wasn't the fool she thought I was. To my son, I leave the pleasure of earning a living; for twenty-five years, he thought the pleasure was mine.'

PAULA Beswick left a fortune to her doctor on condition that he look upon her face once a year as long as he lived. Her embalmed body was kept in the case of a grandfather clock for 111 years.

THE poet Heinrich Heine left his estate to his wife on condition that she remarry, explaining in his will that as a consequence 'there will be at least one man to regret my death'.

A Farewell to Arms – and Other Bits

ALTHOUGH Galileo is buried next to Michaelangelo and Machiavelli in the Church of Santa Croce in Florence, his middle finger is in another part of town, on display at the Museum of the History of Science. It seems that before Galileo was buried, Anton Francesco Gori (a nobleman who was a fanatic admirer of Galileo) cut off three of the astronomer's fingers to keep as relics. Two are in a private collection, while the right middle finger is in the museum.

WHEN Joseph Haydn died in Vienna, his grateful master, Prince Esterházy, wished to have his body returned to Eisenstadt, his home for most of his life, for burial in a suitably grand marble tomb. However, a group of Viennese phrenologists decided that by studying Haydn's skull, they might discover the root of his great talent. Accordingly, Joseph Haydn's body was removed from his temporary resting place, and decapitated.

When it was discovered that Haydn's head had been stolen, the culprit confessed to the crime, but refused to return the head unless Prince Esterházy compensated him. Prince Esterházy would not be blackmailed, so Haydn's headless body was buried.

The head was eventually bequeathed to the Musik Verein museum in Vienna, but it disappeared again. It then reappeared at the home of an Austrian professor, who displayed it on his piano. When the professor died, his widow loaned the head to the Vienna Pathological Museum. The Musik Verein sued for its return. It was returned in 1895 and it stayed in Vienna while the people of Eisenstadt negotiated for its return to Haydn's tomb. Negotiations continued for over forty years, and it finally looked as if the head was going to be returned. Unfortunately, World War II broke out and Haydn's head was not an issue. The war ended with Haydn's head in the Russian Sector of a divided Vienna. Once again the discussions began. In 1954 a satisfactory agreement was reached and Joseph Haydn's head was returned to his body, one hundred and thirty-five years after he died.

WHEN Oliver Cromwell overthrew the British monarchy in 1649, one of the first things he did was have King Charles I beheaded. The king's was then paraded around London on a cart. Cromwell died peacefully in his bed four years later. His body was embalmed, a lavish state funeral took place, and he was interred in Westminster Abbey.

In 1660 Charles II, son of Charles I, restored the monarchy. One of the first things *he* did was have Oliver Cromwell exhumed. His body was dragged through the streets of London to Tyburn, where it was publicly hanged on the gallows, then beheaded. The slipshod executioner used eight strokes of his axe to complete the deed. In the process, he damaged Cromwell's nose as well as some other vital parts of his anatomy. Spiked on a pole, the disfigured head was paraded through the streets and finally housed on the roof of the House of Commons.

One night, twenty-four years later, during a particularly heavy storm, a sentry on duty in front of Parliament was almost knocked out by what he first thought was a cannon ball falling from the sky. He had been hit by Cromwell's head which had been shaken loose by the wind. The sentry wrapped the head up and took it home. It was eventually sold to an itinerant who went from village to village charging people to see it or, for a higher fee, to hold it.

For the next 200 years Cromwell's head continued to travel the country, appearing in the strangest of places: a private museum in London owned by a tycoon called Mr Dupuy; in the hands of a down-and-out actor called Samuel Russell; on sale in Bond Street in 1799; on exhibition at the Royal Archaeological Institute, London, in 1911.

It finally made its way back to Cambridge, Cromwell's alma mater. There, remarkably well preserved, although now missing an ear as well as the nose, it was placed in an oak box, and in a final ceremony, Oliver Cromwell's head was laid to rest in 1960 at his old college, Sydney Sussex. As for the rest of his body, it may turn up someday.

WALTER Raleigh is possibly the only man who lost his head twice. After he was beheaded by Queen Elizabeth I, his head was placed in a red velvet bag and given to his widow. She had it preserved and placed on display in her home. Many years later when their son died he left instructions that the head be buried with him. Unfortunately the head had somehow disappeared, never to be found.

AFTER his death in 1955, Albert Einstein's brain was removed for post-mortem analysis. It was taken to the Princeton Medical Centre in New Jersey, where it was sliced up and sent to specialists around America. One piece was found in the 1970s in an office in Wichita, Kansas – it was in a jar filed in an old cider carton in the corner of the office.

ANOTHER famous brain that strayed is that of President John F. Kennedy. After his post-mortem at John Hopkins Medical Centre in Bethesda, his brain disappeared, and has never been found.

KING Richard II's jawbone was stolen from Westminster Abbey by a naughty schoolboy in 1776. It did not rejoin the rest of the monarch until 1906.

THE heart of the poet and novelist Thomas Hardy is buried in the graveyard of St Michael's Church, Stinsford, Dorset, while the ashes of the rest of him lie in Poets' Corner, in Westminster Abbey. In fact, not only is Hardy's heart buried in Dorset, but the tomb also contains the cat that ate it. It seems that when Hardy's heart was removed, it was placed on a table, in a tin, while his body was being prepared for removal to Westminster. Hardy's cat knocked over the tin and couldn't resist the meal that fell out. Caught in the midst of dinner, the cat was strangled, placed in the tin along with what remained of the heart, and buried in the churchyard.

WHEN Queen Eleanor of Castile, wife of Edward I, died in 1290, her body was removed from Lincolnshire and carried to London for burial in Westminster Abbey. Part of her remained in Lincolnshire however – her bowels were buried in Lincoln.

THE heart of King Louis XIV of France met a most ignoble end. It was bought by a member of the Harcourt family from a grave robber during the French Revolution. They kept it in a snuff box, but one day one of them made the mistake of showing it to Dr William Buckland, the first professor of Geology at Oxford University. Dr Buckland had a great appetite for unusual foods, and prided himself on eating anything – the more curious and exotic the better. As soon as he saw the heart lying there, his salivary glands began to work overtime. He exclaimed, 'I have eaten many things, but never the heart of a king!' and before the horrified Harcourts could protest, he popped the embalmed heart into his mouth and swallowed it.

M OST people know the story of Eva Peron's preserved body being kept by her grief-stricken husband, General Peron, President of Argentina. However, it is not so widely known that his body was subject to a post-mortem adventure too. In 1987, his hands were stolen from his grave, and a ransom note was sent to the current president demanding £5 million for their return.

O NE of the casualties of the battle of Waterloo was the leg of Lord Uxbridge. He was sitting astride his horse, next to the Duke of Wellington, when he was shot in the leg. 'By God, sir, I've lost my leg,' Uxbridge exclaimed. Wellington looked away from the battle just long enough to reply, 'By God, sir, so you have!'

Uxbridge was taken, along with the severed leg, to the home of a local forester named Hyacinth Perres. There the wound was dressed and the seemingly worthless leg was promptly thrown out the window into the garden where it was buried along with the rest of the rubbish. The one-legged Uxbridge returned to England and a hero's welcome.

Some time later, some British tourists knocked on the French forester's door asking to see where Uxbridge's leg had been buried. They were willing to pay to see it. Hyacinth realized there could be an economic opportunity in the buried limb so he dug up the decaying leg, dressed it in a trouser leg and placed it on display attracting paying curiosity seekers for years. He finally had a funeral for the leg with full military honours, attended by Uxbridge, making him perhaps the first person to have attended his own funeral twice – once as a guest and once as a participant.

I N 1983, a tomb containing 20,000 Korean noses was found in Japan by South Korean university professor Kim Moongil. They belonged to troops killed during the Japanese invasion of Korea in 1597, and were taken to Japan as proof of the kills. The noses were officially welcomed home in a special ceremony, presided over by the President of South Korea.

Life After Death

B Y placing the beds of dying patients on scales and noting their weight immediately before and after death, Nils Olof Jacobson, a Swedish doctor, concluded that the human soul weighs twenty-one grams.

A T one time, it was common practice for a finger to be amputated from a corpse just prior to burial. If the deceased did not scream, it was assumed he or she really was dead.

I T is commonly believed that hair and nails continue to grow after death, and some people will go so far as to say they have seen proof of this with their own eyes. In fact, the reason hair and nails are measurably longer a week or so after death is that about one sixteenth of an inch represents hair shaft and nail which was padded by skin while the body lived – this skin gave supporting tissues to both the hair and nails. After death, the tissue collapses and shrinks, thereby revealing the hair shaft and nail base normally concealed.

Odds and Ends

GRAVEDIGGERS in Siberia have a tough job in the winter, trying to bury corpses in the frozen earth. As a remedy they pour paraffin over the frozen ground, set light to it, and when the fire has burnt out, they can dig through the top layer of soil. They continue like this until enough earth has been removed to enable the coffin to be buried.

IN an attempt to prove how imperfect the medical definition of 'brain dead' is, an Ontario neurologist made an EEG analysis of a brain-size mould of lime-flavoured jelly. He obtained readings that could easily have been interpreted as signs of life – the squiggly 'lifelines' being reflected stray electrical signals from nearby respirators, monitors, and even movements of nursing staff.

A MEDICAL student at the University of Alabama had quite a shock when she walked into her dissection class in 1982 – one of the corpses she was to work on was that of her great-aunt.